THE COMPLETE IDIOT'S GUIDE® TO

Dachshunds

by Liz Palika

ALPHA

A member of Penguin Group (USA) Inc.

Copyright © 2003 by Liz Palika

International Standard Book Number: 0-02-864404-2
Library of Congress Catalog Card Number: 2002110192

05   04   03   8   7   6   5   4   3   2

Interpretation of the printing code: The rightmost number of the first series of numbers is the year of the book's printing; the rightmost number of the second series of numbers is the number of the book's printing. For example, a printing code of 02-1 shows that the first printing occurred in 2002.

Printed in the United States of America

Note: This publication contains the opinions and ideas of its author. It is intended to provide helpful and informative material on the subject matter covered. It is sold with the understanding that the author and publisher are not engaged in rendering professional services in the book. If the reader requires personal assistance or advice, a competent professional should be consulted.

The author and publisher specifically disclaim any responsibility for any liability, loss, or risk, personal or otherwise, which is incurred as a consequence, directly or indirectly, of the use and application of any of the contents of this book.

Publisher: *Marie Butler-Knight*
Product Manager: *Phil Kitchel*
Managing Editor: *Jennifer Chisholm*
Acquisitions Editor: *Mike Sanders*
Development Editor: *Jennifer Moore*
Senior Production Editor: *Christy Wagner*
Copy Editor: *Michael Dietsch*
Illustrator: *Chris Eliopoulos*
Cover/Book Designer: *Trina Wurst*
Indexer: *Tonya Heard*
Layout/Proofreading: *Megan Douglass, Becky Harmon*

Permission to reprint the Dachshund Breed Standard in Chapter 2 granted by the Dachshund Club of America.

All photographs by Ed Kelley.

Contents at a Glance

Contents

Foreword

Congratulations on discovering Dachshunds, the most popular of all the small breeds. Their size, color, and coat may vary, but they share one common gene—the gene that gives them the ability to bring a smile to everyone's face!

Dachsies might be small in stature, but they are large in personality, and their looks can be deceiving! If you think you're getting a cute lap dog, you are only half right. Cute yes, but lap dog—maybe not. This little dog was bred to track, scent, and flush out badgers, foxes, and rabbits—a job that encouraged stubbornness, tenaciousness, and independence. So this is no simple lap dog.

Dachshunds are a truly remarkable breed. The short and long body of a Dachsie not only makes them great to look at, but also enables them to be superb athletes and workers. They have the ability to do a variety of activities, from therapy dog, small search and rescue, flyball, agility, trials, watchdog, and best friend, just to name a few.

When considering a Dachsie, plan wisely and do not be impulsive. Stay away from the quick purchase at the mall or corner pet store. Those places only want your credit card. No reputable breeder will ever sell a puppy to a pet store. Research breeders and find a reputable and honest one. A good breeder will want to meet you and will ask you many questions about how you plan to provide and care for your Dachsie. You need to know what your puppies parents are like. Your dog's sound temperament and good health are vital, and these qualities are mostly determined by breeding.

The Complete Idiot's Guide to Dachshunds will prepare you for a relationship with a Dachsie. From housetraining and obedience to being the leader of your Dachsie pack, author Liz Palika, a trainer I respect highly, walks you through the "how-tos" of working with your new dog and shows you the best way to navigate the world of the Dachshund.

When you get a dog, everyone from the mailman to the store clerk will want to give you advice, and although they are usually well meaning, their advice is usually incorrect. Liz Palika is extraordinarily thorough and not only defines every term relative to the Dachshund, but also dispels any myths you might have heard from well-meaning friends and neighbors.

Many things are essential to a good, long relationship with your Dachsie, and training and exercise are two of the most important. Although Dachsie's strong personalities and stubbornness can make obedience a challenging event, the payoff is worth it. And this is not a breed that should be stuck indoors with little possibility to play and work outside. This is a common misconception among many of my clients—often they think that because their dog is small, he doesn't require exercise. Nothing could be farther from the truth. This is not a breed that will be happy being paper-trained, if that means no daily walk. Make sure you are ready for a seven-day-a-week walk, regardless of the weather, how tired you are, your work schedule, or your love life. A dog is a dog; they all need long walks outside daily, and your Dachshund is no exception.

Over my last 16 years as a professional dog trainer and behavioral consultant, I have seen hundreds of Dachshunds privately and in classes. Once you have a Dachsie, you become a member of an "elite" group of people. Dachsie owners so admire their breed that they find endless ways to celebrate them whenever possible. In New York City, there is even an annual Dachshund parade. Hundreds of Dachsie owners get together, gush, admire, boast, and brag about their most prized family members. Dachsies dressed in pearls and leather, cotton and nylon—no matter how they are styled, the personality of this truly one-of-a-kind breed always shines through as a fun, determined, and intelligent dog.

Stacy Alldredge
Owner, Who's Walking Who Dog Obedience and Behavioral Training (212-414-1551; wwwdogs@aol.com)

Introduction

The Complete Idiot's Guide to Dachshunds is a different kind of breed book. This book is going to tell you the good (in fact, wonderful) aspects of owning a Dachsie, but also the bad. There are many breed books available that will tell you that the breed being written about is wonderful, awesome, perfect, and the absolute best choice for everyone! This book is not like those books.

As a dog obedience instructor, I see between 700 and 1,000 dogs and their owners each year in my classes. Many people I work with have done a lot of research before adding a dog to their family yet still find out they really didn't know as much about the breed as they thought. Unfortunately, I see it often with Dachsies. People bring home this adorable, long-eared, long-backed, short-legged puppy with huge eyes, and immediately fall in love. However, when the puppy's paws hit the ground running, they realize the books often don't tell the whole story! Well, this one will!

This book will help you decide whether you even need a dog, or have the time, energy, and money to take care of one. Once you've made the big decision about dog ownership, we decide whether a Dachshund is actually the right dog for you. You may find that a Dachsie sounds perfect for you, or you may decide that a Dachsie would drive you nuts! And if that's the case, it's best to find that out before you bring one home!

Part 2 helps you get started once your bring your new dog home. You'll find out all about housetraining and establishing household rules. Part 3 helps you care for your Dachsie, including some emergency first-aid information. Part 4 guides you through the training process. Even if you decide to enroll in a training class (good idea!), this part will help you and, at the same time, will answer many of your questions concerning canine behavior.

Who Am I?

Most breed books are written by people who have owned, shown, and bred their breed for many years. I am not a Dachsie breeder nor have I shown a Dachsie, so why am I writing this book? Because I see the side of Dachsie ownership that many breeders don't see. As an obedience instructor for pet dog owners, I see the dogs that will never go to a dog show. I see the pet dog owners struggling with a well-loved but challenging dog.

In a recent basic obedience class, a couple attended with their red brindle smooth Dachsie, Tiger, who had never walked on a leash before. When I asked the owners why, they said Tiger didn't like to walk on a leash, so they carried him. This young dog had never, ever gone for a walk—he had always gone for a "carry"! This is not an unusual example of the breed's ability to train their owners.

I have been teaching dog obedience classes for more than 25 years. I have taught all levels of classes, from puppy through basic obedience on through utility. Currently, my focus is on teaching pet owners, so I have been concentrating on puppy, basic, and intermediate-level classes designed to help pet dog owners train their dog to be a companion and friend instead of a pain in the neck.

I also do a lot of therapy dog work, teach therapy dog classes, and am the founder of the Foundation for Pet Provided Therapy. My three dogs and I visit local Alzheimer's facilities, nursing and retirement homes, schools, and hospitals.

My dogs and I have also been involved in many different dog sports and activities through the years, including agility, carting, conformation, Frisbee, flyball, obedience, schutzhund, and search and rescue.

Decoding the Text

You don't need to be an expert on dogs or Dachshunds to understand this book. There will be no technical gibberish of any kind, and in fact, any words that I feel need to be defined, will be! This book is written for people who are thinking of adding a Dachsie to the family, or already have.

You'll find four different kinds sidebars throughout this book, each designed to add some additional information to the text.

Bet You Didn't Know

These tidbits of information may not be earth-shattering, but you'll probably find them helpful and maybe even get a good laugh out of them, too!

Dog Talk

These doggie definitions will make understanding this book a walk in the park.

Watch Out!

Read these boxes for some things to watch out for in order to raise a well-behaved and healthy dog.

Dachsie Wisdom

Obey these commands (okay, they're really just tips) to find out how to be a good Dachsie owner.

Special Thanks to the Technical Reviewer

The Complete Idiot's Guide to Dachshunds was reviewed by two experts who double-checked the accuracy of what you'll learn here to help us ensure that this book gives you everything you need to know about Dachshunds. Special thanks are extended to Deb Eldredge, a dog owner, competitor, and veterinarian, and Beth Adelman, an experienced dog book editor and the former editor of *DogWorld* and the *AKC Gazette*.

Trademarks

All terms mentioned in this book that are known to be or are suspected of being trademarks or service marks have been appropriately capitalized. Alpha Books and Penguin Group (USA) Inc. cannot attest to the accuracy of this information. Use of a term in this book should not be regarded as affecting the validity of any trademark or service mark.

Part **1**

Half a Dog High, Two Dogs Long

Before you bring home a dog, it's important to take a hard look at what's involved in dog ownership and make sure a dog is really the right pet for you. After all, a dog is a big commitment—in time, energy, and money.

If you decide that a dog would be the right pet for you, let's look at Dachshunds. Where did they come from? What was their purpose? We will discover what makes them the kind of dog they are and answer many questions you might have as we discover what makes these dogs so special. However, these unique dogs are not the right dogs for everyone, so let's make sure you and a Dachshund would be a perfect fit before you bring one home.

Once you have decided a Dachsie would suit you perfectly, how do you find one? We'll take a look at breeders and Dachsie rescue, as well as other ways to find a dog. You'll also find out how to choose the individual dog to suit your needs.

The Dachshund you choose will be with you for the next 12 to 14 years, so let's make sure you choose the right dog for you.

Many Dachshund owners say their dog is "half a dog high and two dogs long!"

Is a Dachshund the Right Dog for You?

In This Chapter

- 🏠 The responsibilities of owning a dog
- 🏠 Gauging your energy and time
- 🏠 The pros and cons of dog ownership
- 🏠 Dachshund personality traits

Dachshunds, often called "*Dachsies*" or "*Doxies*," have been extremely popular for many years. The American Kennel Club's (AKC) statistics for 2001 showed Dachshunds are the fourth most popular dog, with more than 50,000 dogs registered. Only Labrador Retrievers, Golden Retrievers, and German Shepherd Dogs are more popular. Dachshund popularity isn't a new thing, though, and in fact, the number of registered dogs has remained quite consistent. The AKC's registration figures from 1997 through 2001 averaged 50,000 to 54,000 Dachshunds each year.

Dachshund people, like their dogs, are a breed apart, although it's hard to say exactly what a Dachshund owner is like. It's not money, although money is needed to care for the dog. It's not social status—either high or low! It's not professions or occupations; people in all walks of life have Dachsies. Instead, Dachshund ownership seems to be more a state of mind. People who love Dachsies like to have fun and like to socialize with other Dachsie owners. But beware! Dachshund owners rarely stop at owning just one Dachsie!

Dog Ownership Is a Responsibility

Before you jump in with both feet and bring home a Dachsie, let's decide whether dog ownership is even right for you. Too many dogs, even Dachsies, end up in shelters or rescued because the people who brought them home weren't prepared for dog ownership (see Chapter 4 for more on shelters and Dachsie rescue programs). Dog ownership requires responsibility on your part. This furry life will depend on you for all his care for 12 to 14 years. Are you willing to take on that responsibility? Don't assume other members of the family—

Dog Talk

The breed is called **Dachshund** (pronounced *DOCK-sund*) or **Dachsie.** "Doxie" has been used for years but is now considered somewhat disrespectful.

especially kids—will shoulder the responsibility for the dog. One person must take primary responsibility. If too many people are involved, it's too easy for each to assume that someone else will take care of the dog, and the dog will be the one to suffer.

To help you decide whether a Dachshund—or any dog—is the right pet for you, let's take a look at your previous pets. Have you owned a dog before? Did that dog live his entire life with you? If he did, awesome! If he didn't, why not? Was he too much work? Was he misbehaved? Did you not have time to train him? Have you owned any other pets? Cats, rabbits, hamsters, tropical fish? Did those pets live out their lives with you? Did you faithfully keep the litter box, cage, or aquarium clean?

If you have owned pets previously and were willing to do what was necessary to keep them healthy and happy, and the pets lived out their lives with you, dog ownership might well be the right choice for you. However, if you have a habit of giving up a pet when things get tough, or if you get bored cleaning litter boxes, cages, or fish tanks, then please rethink the idea of getting a dog.

Watch Out!

Dog ownership isn't just walks on the beach; it is also daily, mundane chores that must be done. Ask yourself whether you can and will do those chores.

The popularity of Dachshunds has remained stable for the past decade.

How Busy Are You?

A dog will require a great deal of your time. In the first few days, your dog—especially a puppy—will be lonely and possibly afraid.

You and other family members will need to spend time with the dog to reassure him that he is loved and safe. But you will need to spend time with your dog after those first few days, too. Daily care takes time.

Bonding with the dog also takes time. This time is well spent, however, as the bond between a dog and owner is something unique and special. But this bond doesn't happen automatically; it takes time to develop.

A dog will require a great deal of your time.

Housetraining takes time, as does teaching the household rules. You'll need to supervise your dog as he gets to know the house so he doesn't get into trouble, destroy stuff, or hurt himself.

Training will require your time, too. All dogs need to learn the basic obedience commands such as Sit, Down, Stay, Come, and Heel. And you'll need to take time to learn how to implement those commands around the house and maybe even enroll in a dog training class.

Of course, you'll also need to take the time to play with your dog and have fun with him. Exercise takes time, too, and so does grooming. As your dog grows up, you will spend less time housetraining and supervising your dog, but you may decide to participate in some dog sports or activities. Many Dachsies are excellent therapy dogs, and—you guessed it—that requires time, too!

So take an honest look at your life and decide if you have the time to spend with a dog. If you just have 10 minutes here and 20 minutes there, that won't do. A dog, and especially a Dachsie, will be extremely unhappy if left alone for many hours each and every day. A dog needs your time, your attention, and your companionship.

Pets Aren't Cheap

Besides needing your time, a dog will also require a financial commitment from you. A dog from a breeder may make a dent in your wallet, although a Dachsie from rescue may be only a modest investment. However, every dog should go see the veterinarian right after you bring him home, and that will cost some money. Plus, the shopping you'll do for your dog—dog food, bowls, a crate, a leash, a collar, and dog toys—will also take some of your hard-earned cash. You may also need to build a dog run or make some repairs to your fence so your Dachsie can't get out.

These initial expenses are usually one-time-only expenses, at least until toys are worn out and a collar is outgrown, but other expenses are ongoing. Dog food isn't cheap, especially good-quality food. Your dog should see the veterinarian on a regular basis as a puppy to get his vaccinations, then yearly for a checkup and booster vaccines. He'll also need to visit the vet to be neutered or spayed.

What about emergencies? Do you have some savings or a credit card that you can set aside in case of pet emergencies? Veterinarians who work in emergency clinics all have heart-breaking stories of dog owners faced with an emergency who don't have the money to pay for the needed care. The dogs either have to go without or are euthanized. Make sure you have the financial ability to care for your dog before you bring him home!

Got a Lot of Energy?

If you've never had a dog, you probably have no idea how a dog will change your life. I tell my dog training class students that I haven't gone to the bathroom alone in years. I always have three dog faces peering in at me, watching to see if I'm okay and how long I will be sitting there! If I'm there for a moment, one will snuggle up for petting. I always have a dog or two or three by my side, at my feet, or following me around. But that's dog ownership!

Dachshunds are full of energy. Can you keep up with one?

If you have a dog, you'll need the energy to do all that your dog needs, including all his care, play, exercise, and need for companionship. A dog needs to be walked daily, or if you live in a condo or apartment, several times a day.

Dachsie Wisdom

Dachshund puppies are a bundle of energy! They love to run, chase, chew, dig, and explore. If you are going to bring home a puppy, make sure you have the energy to deal with puppy antics.

Patience Is a Virtue

All dogs need training, especially Dachsies! An untrained Dachsie can be a terror, and an untrained, spoiled Dachsie is a brat! However, Dachsies don't always make training easy; they can be stubborn, hardheaded, and exasperating when they want to be. Do you have the energy, persistence, and patience to train a dog, especially a Dachsie?

The Good and the Not So Good

As a child, I read all the classic dog books. I loved Lad and all the Sunnybrook Collies. I cried when the dogs died in *Where the Red Fern Grows*. Lassie and Rin Tin Tin were my heroes, and I knew when I grew up I wanted a dog just like Rin Tin Tin. When I got my first dog (a Dachsie, by the way!), I was heartbroken to discover that Lassie's escapades and heroism were all Hollywood mythology!

There is not a flesh-and-bone dog alive who can live up to the adventures and bravery of Hollywood's dogs. Oh, that isn't to say there aren't some awesome canine heroes out there; there are, and they all have my respect and admiration. However, even those heroes aren't Lassie or Rin Tin Tin.

But that doesn't make dog ownership any less exciting. It's just different. So why should we own dogs? Well, as with anything else, there are both good points and not-so-good points to owning a dog.

The Good:

- A dog is a wonderful companion. You're never really alone when you have a dog.

- A dog is a good listener and never reveals secrets.

- A dog is great therapy.

- A dog will love you unconditionally with all his heart.

- People who love and live with dogs are healthier than people who live alone.

- A dog needs playtime, exercise, and walks and will bring you with him.

- You'll meet other people when you have a dog, especially when you have a Dachsie.

- A dog will warn you of trespassers and increase your sense of security.

- A dog will make you laugh.

The Not So Good:

- Dogs do require a financial investment on your part.

- Dogs can be messy and destructive.

- Dogs require your time and energy.

- You can't be quite as spontaneous when you own a dog; you have responsibilities.

- You'll suffer emotionally when your dog grows old and passes away.

The Good Outweighs the Not So Good

I'm a dog owner, have always had dogs, and can't imagine life without dogs, so I'm not really a fair judge of dog ownership. I can put up with the not-so-good aspects of owning a dog because I really enjoy the positives!

> **Dachsie Wisdom** _____
>
> During the September 11 tragedy in New York City, I sat on the sofa in my living room watching the television and cried, as did so many other people. However, as I cried, one of my dogs, Riker, was licking the tears off my face, Kes was snuggled up to me as close as she could get, and my third dog, Dax, was bringing me all her toys. I'm sure in her mind she felt that the toys made her happy, so perhaps they would make me happy, too! As devastated as I was, at least my dogs were there to comfort me!

But just because dog ownership is right for me doesn't mean it's right for you. Think through all the good points and the not-so-good points. Take a look—a hard look—at your budget and decide if you can afford a dog. Make sure you have the time and energy. And then decide if you, and all the other members of your family, will enjoy having a dog.

> **Watch Out!** _____
>
> The average cost for raising a puppy from eight weeks to one year of age is about $1,000, and that does not include the puppy's purchase price!

Do You Know a Dachshund?

Okay, so you've made it this far and have decided that you can afford a dog and will be able to handle the responsibility of dog ownership. You have the time and energy to do what's needed, and you even think you would like living with a dog. Awesome! Now what? Is a Dachshund the right dog for you, or would you be better off with a Labrador Retriever or a Poodle?

First of all, if you know someone with a Dachshund, spend some time with their dog. Ask to take the dog for a walk or two, go to the park for a picnic, or even ask to borrow the dog for a few hours here and there. Offer to pet-sit for the weekend when the owners are out of town. Spend some time with the dog and get to know him. If you know several Dachshunds, spend time with several of them, as each has his or her own personality.

By getting to know several dogs, you'll have a better understanding of what a Dachsie is, especially if you have owned dogs of other breeds before, because Dachsies are different!

The Affectionate Dachsie

Dachsies aren't always overly demonstrative, as are some other breeds of dogs. A Golden Retriever shows he loves his owner with every fiber of his being, but a Dachshund isn't as extroverted. If you have a Dachsie, you know you're loved, but it's often a little more subtle.

Watch Out!
Many neighbors don't appreciate a barking dog. Talk to your neighbors before you bring home a Dachsie.

The Protective Dachsie

Dachsies fancy themselves as super guard dogs and can sometimes take this role too far. Whereas a Rottweiler might bark when someone tries to climb over the fence, a Dachsie will probably warn away anyone within 100 feet of the fence in any direction!

The Courageous Dachsie

Badgers are tough, ferocious fighters, and Dachsies used to hunt badgers, so they had to be equally tough. Dachsies today, even city dogs who've never smelled a badger, retain that courageous temperament. Dachsies don't realize they are small dogs and won't hesitate to take on or challenge a much larger dog, trespasser, or other real or imagined enemy. This can often get them into trouble!

The Manipulative Dachsie

Dachsies, even (or especially!) as puppies, learn how to manipulate their owners. Dachsies know they are loved and don't hesitate to take advantage of it! A sad look gets an extra throw of the ball, while a sad, begging look can get a tidbit from the table. A wiggling body and wagging tail will get an owner out of the armchair and out for a walk. Dachsies know what they want and will do anything to get it!

The Too-Smart Dachsie

Any dog trainer will tell you that Dachsies are too smart for their own good! They are smart enough to get into trouble—but smart doesn't necessarily mean obedient.

The Obedient Dachsie

Snicker, snicker, snort, snort. Okay, now, that's enough. Dachsies can be obedient when they want to be—or if the *motivation* is good enough. That's where the owner's training skills come into play!

> **Dog Talk**
>
> **Motivation,** or a motivator, is something the dog is willing to work for, often a toy or a treat.

The Food-Motivated Dachsie

Okay, this is where Dachsies prevail! Dachsies are food-motivated; often so much so that they turn into food thieves and trash can raiders. Dachsies like, no, *love* food! That can aid in training, as food is a good training motivator. However, their love of food can also lead to obesity, which is very bad for that long Dachsie back.

The Hunting Dachsie

Never, ever forget that the Dachshund was originally bred as a hunter—a tough hunter! Badgers are formidable opponents.

Anything smaller than a Dachshund (or even slightly larger) could be considered fair prey, and that includes cats who run away, rabbits (wild or domestic), ferrets, mice, rats, hamsters, gerbils, chinchillas, and any other small prey or pets.

> **Bet You Didn't Know**
> The hunting instinct is triggered by movement. If a cat or rabbit sits still and doesn't move, the Dachsie might not chase it. However, if the cat or rabbit runs, the prey drive kicks in and the Dachsie will be off in hot pursuit!

Think About It

Do these characteristics sound like ones you would enjoy in a dog? If you don't think you could tolerate them, don't get a Dachsie. If you think you'll be able to change these characteristics, you're wrong; get another breed instead. However, if you think you would enjoy a dog with these traits, awesome! Welcome to the wonderful, weird, wacky world of Dachshunds!

The Least You Need to Know

- Take a hard look at yourself and make sure you're ready for the responsibility of dog ownership.
- Make sure you have the financial means to buy and care for the dog, including unexpected emergencies.
- A dog will require a great deal of your time and energy on a daily basis.
- Before you bring home a Dachshund, get to know one or two and discover what they are all about. They are unique.

2

What Is a Dachshund?

In This Chapter

- 🏠 The origins of the Dachshund
- 🏠 Dachsies come to the USA
- 🏠 The AKC Dachshund standard
- 🏠 Dachshunds today

Almost everyone can identify a Dachshund; he's the dog with the long body and short legs. Most people can even differentiate between other long-bodied dogs such as Basset Hounds and Corgis. But what makes a Dachshund a Dachshund?

Breed registries such as the American Kennel Club (AKC) have what is called a breed standard for each recognized breed. The standard is a written description of the "perfect" or ideal dog of that breed. At conformation dog shows, judges compare the dogs competing on that day to the AKC description to choose the best dog. Breeders can also use the standard to analyze potential breeding stock.

A breed is much more than its physical attributes, however, although with some breeds—such as the Dachshund—those physical attributes are very unique! A breed is also its history, what it was bred to do (its purpose), and its personality and temperament. So let's see what makes Dachshunds so different from other dogs.

The Origins of the Breed

Long-bodied, short-legged dogs have been known throughout history. Egyptian tomb drawings show dogs with these characteristics, although they look nothing like today's Dachshunds. However, skeletons of dogs similar to today's Dachshunds have been found in the northern Czech Republic and in Roman ruins in Germany.

Most Dachshund historians believe that Dachshunds are descendants of the now-extinct St. Hubert Hound. This breed, named for its originator St. Hubert (656 to 727 C.E.), was known for its excellent scenting abilities and long, low body.

> **Dachsie Wisdom**
>
> Many Dachsie owners call their dogs "carpet sharks" for their speed, strength, and ability to find the tiniest bit of dropped food!

> **Dog Talk**
>
> **Go to ground trials** give Dachsies a chance to enter an artificial tunnel to find and confront a safely caged prey animal.

The breed as we know it today was developed in Germany by farmers, foresters, and hunters. In the 1600s and 1700s, these working men wanted a dog capable of tracking and scenting game but also able to "go to ground" (enter animal burrows and dens). The dog also had to be able to hold his prey and bark loud enough and long enough for the hunter to catch up and dispatch the prey.

As the breed became more developed, they also developed specialties. The larger-size Dachsies (30 to 35 pounds) hunted badgers. Badgers were a constant threat to farmers' livestock, and packs of tenacious Dachsies would be sent down the badger holes to corner and take out these strong animals.

Medium-size Dachshunds (16 to 24 pounds) were used to hunt small predators and pests, including foxes. The smallest Dachshunds (10 pounds or less) were used to flush weasels or rabbits from their holes.

Bet You Didn't Know

Badgers are stout, short legged, about 25 inches long, and weigh about 20 to 25 pounds. When cornered or frightened, they can be very aggressive and can be a formidable opponent.

There's a Reason for That Shape

The Dachshund's slim body and short legs made it easier for the dog to fit down the tunnels, burrows, and dens of his prey. The legs, although short, were powerful enough to dig to enlarge holes when needed and strong enough to give the dog leverage when fighting his prey.

Dachsies were bred to be hunters, and those instincts remain strong.

If the Dachshund's body was in proportion to his leg length, he would be a very small dog and unable to do the work needed. Therefore, the breed has a relatively large but slim body for his leg length. This gives ample room for internal organs, and enough musculature for the dog to do his work.

Dachsie Wisdom

A healthy Dachshund should be fit and well muscled with muscles easily seen and felt under the skin.

When petting one, many people unacquainted with Dachshunds comment on the dog's muscular build. When fit, Dachsies are well muscled—they had to be to hunt. This breed was not designed to be a couch potato!

There's a Reason for That Personality

When asked to describe their dog's personality, some Dachshund owners say their dog is sweet, loving, and affectionate, while others say their dog is curious and intelligent. Almost all, however, will mention the words *eager, intense, stubborn, hard-headed, focused,* and *feisty.* A dog who used to hunt badgers or foxes had to be focused, intense, feisty, courageous, and stubborn. If the dog wasn't, the prey could overwhelm the dog or escape. Early enthusiasts of the breed described the temperament as snappy, pugnacious, tenacious, brave, and quarrelsome. All these personality traits, when combined with the breed's physical attributes, made it the prized and successful hunter it was designed to be.

Dachsies Come to the USA

Dachshunds were introduced to the United States more than a century and a half ago, many arriving in the mid-1800s with German immigrants. In 1885, the Dachshund Club of America was formed, and the breed was recognized by the AKC. The breed immediately became a favorite with dog owners, going from twenty-sixth in registration rankings in 1930 to sixth in 1940. Early American Dachshund enthusiasts included Noel Coward and Clark Gable.

Although Dachsie fanciers enjoyed this popularity, some were worried that the breed might be going "soft," because the conformation show dogs and pet dogs rarely, if ever, hunted. To remedy this problem, some fanciers instituted *field trials* with rules initially patterned after German field trial rules. The U.S. Dachshund Field Trial Club held its first trial in 1935 in Lamington, New Jersey. Dachsies were put to ground and encouraged to enter artificial rabbit burrows. Titles were offered for competition, with the best dogs competing for the coveted Field Trial Champion.

> **Dog Talk**
>
> **Field trials** test the dog's natural hunting abilities and willingness to enter a tunnel or burrow.

Dachshunds may be short of leg but are wonderful athletes just the same.

The AKC Standard for the Dachshund

The AKC standard for the Dachshund is the official written description of the ideal or perfect dog of this breed. Conformation dog show judges look at the dogs competing at each dog show and compare those dogs to each other and to the standard to choose the best dog competing on that day. Dachshund breeders use the standard as a guide to choose the best dogs for their breeding programs. The standard is what keeps a Dachshund looking like a Dachshund … and not a Greyhound!

This description is broken down into several parts. Let's take a look at each part and then discuss it. Try to picture each description in your mind as it is described, and fit the pieces together like a jigsaw puzzle.

> **General Appearance:** Low to the ground, long in body and short of leg with robust muscular development, the skin is elastic and pliable without excessive wrinkling. Appearing neither crippled, awkward, nor cramped in his capacity for movement, the Dachshund is well-balanced with bold and confident head carriage and intelligent, alert facial expression. His hunting spirit, good nose, loud tongue and distinctive build make him well suited for below-ground work and for beating the bush. His keen nose gives him an advantage over most other breeds for trailing. Note: Inasmuch as the Dachshund is a hunting dog, scars from honorable wounds shall not be considered a fault.

This paragraph describes the overall look of the breed, with the long body and short legs, and the bold attitude all Dachsie fanciers know. It's interesting to note that this paragraph also stresses the hunting characteristics of the breed, including the breed's tenacity—described as "spirit"—and barking—described as "loud tongue"! The desire to continue the breed's hunting abilities can also be seen in the last sentence, where scars are not to be penalized.

> **Size, Proportion, Substance:** Bred and shown in two sizes, standard and miniature, miniatures are not a separate classification but compete in a class division for "11 pounds and under at 12 months of age and older." Weight of the standard size is usually between 16 and 32 pounds.

> **Bet You Didn't Know** _____
> Most breeds have a preferred head carriage position.
> The Dachshund standard asks for a "head up" position,
> calling it a "bold and confident" position. However, Border
> Collies, for example, are a herding breed with a strong eye (or
> stare) and work with their head much lower, often lower even
> than their shoulders.

This description tells us that standard Dachsies, when full grown, are normally more than 16 pounds and miniature Dachsies are less than 11 pounds.

Head: Viewed from above or from the side, the head tapers uniformly to the tip of the nose. The eyes are of medium size, almond-shaped and dark rimmed, with an energetic, pleasant expression; not piercing; very dark in color. The bridge bones over the eyes are strongly prominent. Wall eyes, except in the case of dappled dogs, are a serious fault. The ears are set near the top of the head, not too far forward, of moderate length, rounded, not narrow, pointed, or folded. Their carriage when animated is with the forward edge just touching the cheek so that the ears frame the face. The skull is slightly arched, neither too broad nor too narrow, and slopes gradually with little perceptible stop into the finely formed, slightly arched muzzle. Black is the preferred color of the nose. Lips are tightly stretched, well covering the lower jaw. Nostrils well open. Jaws opening wide and hinged well back of the eyes, with strongly developed bones and teeth. Teeth: Powerful canine teeth fit closely together in a scissors bite. An even bite is a minor fault. Any other deviation is a serious fault.

This paragraph goes into great detail about how the head should be shaped as well as such details as the expression of the eyes and the hinge of the jaw. Almost all these details are related to the breed's original function. For example, the energetic expression of

___ **Dog Talk** ___

The **stop** is the part of the head where the skull meets the muzzle at or just below the eyes. A **dewlap** is loose skin under the chin and neck, much like a second chin.

the eyes shows the dog's alertness, while the prominent bridge bones over the eyes help protect the eyes. The jaws, which open wide and are hinged far back, enable a hunting dog to grab his prey, and the strong canine teeth allow him to hold his prey and dispatch it.

Neck: Long, muscular, clean-cut, without dewlap, slightly arched in the nape, flowing gracefully into the shoulders.

This sentence is fairly simple and self-explanatory.

Trunk: The trunk is long and fully-muscled. When viewed in profile, the back lies in the straightest possible line between the withers and the short, very slightly arched loin. A body that hangs loosely between the shoulders is a serious fault. Abdomen: Slightly drawn up.

This says that the Dachsie's body should be long (as compared to most other breeds) yet well muscled. The top of the back from the point of the shoulders to the point of the hips should be level and straight. The tummy should be slightly tucked up or, in other words, the dog should have a nice waistline! Again, all of this relates to the dog's physical soundness and ability to do his job.

___ **Dog Talk** ___

The **withers** is the top point of the shoulders where the back of the neck meets the top of the back.

Forequarters: For effective underground work, the front must be strong, deep, long and cleanly muscled.

This, too, like so much in the Dachsie standard, makes reference to the dog's ancestral occupation.

Forequarters in detail: Chest—The breastbone is strongly prominent in front so that on either side a depression or dimple appears. When viewed from the front, the thorax appears oval and extends downward to the mid-point of the forearm. The enclosing structure of well-sprung ribs appears full and oval to allow by its ample capacity, complete development of heart and lungs. The keel merges gradually to the line of the abdomen and extends well beyond the front legs. Viewed in profile, the lowest point of the breast line is covered by the front legs.

This paragraph goes into a lot of detail as to the shape of the chest. The writers of the standard obviously believed that the shape of the chest was important for the front legs to be placed properly (as you will see in upcoming paragraphs) and so that the heart and lungs could be fully developed so they could function correctly.

Shoulder blades: Long, broad, well-laid back and firmly placed upon the well-developed thorax, closely fitted at the withers, furnished with hard yet pliable muscles.

This is a continuation of the description of the chest, as the shoulder blades are fitted to the chest and the next descriptions—of the parts of the front legs—ties the front of the dog together like a canine jigsaw puzzle.

Front legs: Upper arm—Ideally the same length as the shoulder blade and at right angle to the latter, strong of bone and hard of muscle, lying close to the ribs, with elbows close to the body, yet capable of free movement. Forearm—Short, supplied with hard yet pliable muscles on the front and outside, with tightly stretched tendon on the inside and at the back, slightly curved inwards. The joints between the forearms and the feet (wrists) are closer together than the shoulder joints, so that the front does not appear absolutely straight. Knuckling over is a disqualifying fault. Feet—Front paws are full, tight, compact, with well-arched toes and tough, thick pads. They may be equally inclined a trifle outward. There are five toes, four in use close together with a pronounced arch and strong, short nails. Front dewclaws may be removed.

This paragraph describes a short yet powerful front leg made for work. The repeated use of *muscles* and *pliable* and *free movement* show that the writers of this standard wanted to keep the breed a powerful digger; a necessary task for a hunter who goes into burrows. Yet they also wanted the breed to be able to run, twist, turn, and retain a full range of motion in the front legs.

Hindquarters: Strong and cleanly muscled. The pelvis, the thigh, the second thigh, and the metatarsus are ideally the same length and form a series of right angles. From the rear, the thighs are strong and powerful. The legs turn neither in nor out. Metatarsus—Short and strong, perpendicular to the second thigh bone. When viewed from behind, they are upright and parallel. Feet—Hind paws—Smaller than the front paws with four compactly closed and arched toes with tough, thick pads. The entire foot points straight ahead and is balanced equally on the ball and not merely on the toes. Rear dewclaws should be removed. Croup—Long, rounded and full, sinking slightly towards the tail. Tail—Set in continuation of the spine, extending without kinks, twists, or pronounced curvature, and not carried too gaily.

This continues the discussion of a powerful hunter and an athletic dog. The hindquarters may not appear as big and powerful as the forequarters (with the breed's deep chest), but the hindquarters should do more than simply hold up the back end of the body.

Gait: Fluid and smooth. Forelegs reach well forward, without much lift, in unison with the driving action of hind legs. The correct shoulder assembly and well-fitted elbows allow the long, free stride in front. Viewed from the front, the legs do not move in exact parallel planes, but incline slightly inward to compensate for shortness of leg and width of chest. Hind legs drive on a line with the forelegs, with hocks (metatarsus) turning neither in nor out. The propulsion of the hind leg depends on the dog's ability to carry the hind leg to complete extension. Viewed in profile, the forward reach of the hind leg equals the rear extension. The thrust of correct movement is seen when the rear pads are clearly exposed during rear extension. Feet must travel parallel to the line of motion with no tendency to swing out, cross over, or interfere with each other. Short, choppy movement, rolling or high stepping gait, close or overly wide coming or going are incorrect. The Dachshund must have agility, freedom of movement, and endurance to do the work for which he was developed.

This paragraph is self-explanatory; these dogs are (or should be) athletes. The last sentence ties it all together.

Temperament: The Dachshund is clever, lively and courageous to the point of rashness, persevering in above and below ground work, with all the senses well-developed. Any display of shyness is a serious fault.

Watch Out! Some Dachsies in recent years have had shy personalities, a serious fault according to the standard. Unfortunately, these dogs often progress to biting and snapping. These dogs should not be bred and should be handled carefully under the guidance of a trainer or behaviorist.

Potential Dachsie owners should heed this paragraph well!

The balance of the Dachshund breed standard describes the special characteristics of the three coat varieties found in this breed, along with the colors. This will be discussed in detail in Chapter 3. The final paragraph of the standard states:

The foregoing description is that of the ideal Dachshund. Any deviation from the above described dog must be penalized to the extent of the deviation, keeping in mind the importance of the contribution of the various features toward the basic original purpose of the breed.

In other words, it must always be kept in mind that the Dachshund was and must remain a "go to ground" hunting dog.

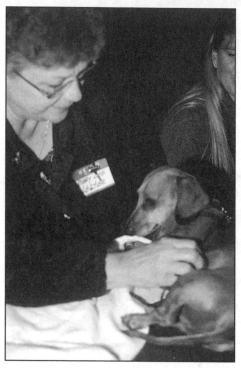

Dachshund popularity remains high. This little breed is extremely appealing to many people.

What Does This Mean to You?

Many dog owners assume that unless they want a show dog, the standard isn't important, but that isn't true at all. If you have fallen in love with this appealing breed, the standard should be important to you.

Good breeders use the standard as a guide to breeding good dogs. Potential breeding stock is compared to the standard, and dogs who best compare to the standard are bred. Dogs whose traits combined could potentially create even better offspring are bred, too.

People who buy a purebred dog do so because they like that breed and they want to know what they are getting. By adhering to a standard and by breeding (ideally) the best of the best of that breed, buyers know what they are bringing home. A Dachshund from a reputable breeder who uses the AKC standard as a guide will look like a Dachsie, not a Basset Hound, and will have the Dachsie personality, not a Poodle personality.

However, not everyone cares about the breed standard. If that's your attitude, you might be just as happy adopting a homeless Dachsie at the shelter or even a Dachsie mix. It's your choice.

Dachshunds Today

As the AKC registration statistics show, Dachshunds have been and remain very popular. Averaging more than 50,000 dogs registered per year, Dachsies rank in popularity behind only Labrador Retrievers, Golden Retrievers, and German Shepherds. The miniatures, in particular, seem to appeal to many people, although the breed's playfulness and high activity level is also quite attractive.

Dachshunds today participate in many dog sports and activities. Although they may not be competitive in some—such as jumping high for a Frisbee—they can still have fun! Some dog sports and activities that Dachshunds have participated in include the following:

- 🏠 **Agility.** A fast-moving, athletic sport in which the dog jumps over different types of jumps, runs through tunnels, and climbs obstacles, all against a time clock.

- 🏠 **Carting.** A noncompetitive activity in which dogs are taught to pull wagons or carts. (Dachsies, of course, would pull a small one!)

🏠 **Conformation dog shows.** Competitions in which dogs compete against others of their breed to win points toward a breed championship. Winners then compete against other breed winners for Best in Show.

🏠 **Flyball.** A competitive relay race sport. Dogs run down a path, jump four hurdles, trigger a wall that tosses a tennis ball, then return the way they came. It is fast and great fun.

🏠 **"Go to ground" Dachshund field trials.** Dogs are introduced to a man-made (or artificial) tunnel to see if they have the instincts to follow the tunnel to find a safely caged rat. This is a test of the dog's natural instincts.

🏠 **Obedience.** Obedience training is for all dogs; however, if you and your dog enjoy training, you may also wish to compete in obedience. Dogs are trained and then compete performing a set of exercises at various levels, from beginning obedience to advanced.

🏠 **Small space disaster search and rescue (often called urban search and rescue).** Most people think of German Shepherds or Bloodhounds when they think of search-and-rescue dogs, but small dogs can be wonderful at small space disaster search and rescue. A small dog can wiggle into places a large dog cannot.

🏠 **Therapy dog work.** Trained dogs who like people are evaluated and certified and then visit people in nursing homes and hospitals. This is a very rewarding activity.

🏠 **Tracking.** Dogs use their natural scenting abilities to follow a set track. This can be competitive, to earn titles, or can be used in search and rescue work.

Although not every dog is a show dog, Dachshund breeders have, for the most part, stayed pretty close to the standard. Most Dachsies today are athletes when given a chance and love to run, chase, jump, and play. Although some shyness has been seen in the breed, most Dachsies show the preferred alert, courageous, and tenacious personality. Hopefully, careful breeding in the future will continue in these lines, and this breed will remain true to its standard and ancestors for years to come.

The Least You Need to Know

- 🐾 The Dachshund originated in Germany as a hunter of burrowing and denning animals.

- 🐾 The AKC Dachshund standard describes the perfect or ideal mental and physical characteristics.

- 🐾 The Dachshund today is still a feisty, courageous, and athletic hunting dog.

- 🐾 A Dachshund is well suited to many canine activities.

Chapter 3

The Many Varieties of Dachshunds

In This Chapter

- A long look at that long body
- The differences between standards and minis
- Smooth, longhaired, and wirehaired coats
- The many colors of Dachsies

Many people really enjoy the Dachshund's high activity level and alert, courageous, and tenacious personality, but they usually don't get to know that side of a Dachsie until after they meet one. What attracts most people to a Dachsie first is the dog's appearance.

The clean-cut, long-bodied profile of a Dachshund is unique. Even the other long-bodied breeds (and there are several different long-bodied breeds) don't have the same appearance as the Dachshund. Each breed was designed for a different purpose and has been bred under a different standard.

When the Dachshund's three coat varieties—smooth, longhaired, and wirehaired—are combined with the various acceptable colors and the two sizes, well, the possibilities are endless. There is, without exaggeration, a Dachshund for every lover of the breed.

A Long Look at That Long Body

The Dachshund's long body is one of her most distinctive characteristics. Unfortunately, it can also be a source of heartbreak; back problems (especially herniated disks) are not unusual in Dachsies. One in four Dachshunds will suffer from some form of disc disease during their lifetimes.

Let's look at the human back first as a means of comparison. People stand and walk upright, with the spine curving gently. The legs absorb the initial shock of movement, but not all of it. The lower regions of the spine absorb the remaining shocks. In people, the most common area for damaged discs is in the lower part of the back. These damaged discs can press on nerve roots, but most of the time don't press upon the spinal cord itself. In people then, herniated discs can cause considerable pain, but rarely result in paralysis.

Bet You Didn't Know

Basset Hounds and Corgis are, other than Dachsies, two of the most popular and well-known long-bodied breeds. Bassets are also hunting dogs, whereas Corgis were bred to herd livestock.

Watch Out!

Herniated discs are not the only back problems Dachsies can suffer from. Problems may range from as minor as a pulled or strained muscle to as severe as a broken back.

In dogs, the back is suspended between the shoulders and hips. The jarring forces, rather than coming up in a straight line from the legs, happen at a right angle to the back. For example, when the dog jumps down from a height, such as from the sofa, the force jars the front legs, which transmit the force to the spine from an angle. This stresses the spine and creates greater compression on the discs. A herniated disc (or discs, as multiple damaged discs are not uncommon) can cause considerable pain and, when pressing upon the spinal cord, even paralysis to the hind legs.

Preventing Back Problems

Dachshund experts recommend that Dachsie puppies be taught from an early age that jumping isn't allowed, especially jumping off furniture, out of the car (especially a pick-up or SUV), or from other high (from the dog's perspective) things. Reasonable jumping—such as small obstacles in the field or low-agility jumps—are allowed as long as the dog has shown no symptoms of back problems previously.

Keeping the dog's weight down will also help prevent back problems. An obese Dachsie is much more likely to hurt himself than a slim dog. Dachsies don't have to be emaciated; that's unhealthy, too. However, keeping the Dachsie slim and fit is important for a healthy back.

Dachsie Wisdom

Dachsies are athletic dogs and shouldn't be couch potatoes just to avoid potential back problems. A fit dog is more likely to be a strong, healthy dog, so just limit excessive jumping, especially jumping down from things.

Don't Make the Back a Problem

When you are deciding whether a Dachsie would be the right dog for you, the breed's long back must be taken into consideration. However, reasonable care can prevent a lot of problems, so don't think you'll have to worry about the dog's back all the time.

The Differences Between Standards and Minis

As noted in Chapter 2, miniature Dachshunds are 11 pounds and under when 1 year of age and over. Standard Dachshunds are usually between 16 and 32 pounds. Although that may not seem like a big difference—after all, there is only 5 pounds difference between 11 and 16 pounds—there is a considerable size difference between the two.

Standard Dachsies have bigger, heavier legs and heavier bones, and are proportionately bigger. The miniatures are finer boned and appear more delicate. There are also a few other differences.

Standards:

- 🏠 Standards are sturdier and do well in rougher situations, such as a rural home where there are fields to romp in and rabbits to chase.

- 🏠 Standards, being sturdier, also do better with younger children. For kids under 10 years of age, a standard is usually better.

- 🏠 Standards like to do things. If you want a Dachsie to go to ground, go for long walks, play flyball, or even pull a little red wagon, a standard is your partner!

- 🏠 Standards really are a big dog on short legs. They have a big dog "can-do" attitude.

Watch Out!

Miniature Dachshund puppies are very tiny. They can easily be injured if inadvertently stepped on, dropped, or sat on.

Miniatures:

- 🏠 Miniatures are funny! They are clowns and love to play to a crowd. These are the dogs for trick training and fun activities.

🏠 Miniatures are great for people who are housebound or unable to get out for exercise, for seniors, and for therapy dog work.

🏠 Miniatures can be more noisy than standards and can be quite high pitched (and annoying) at times.

The In-Between Size

Okay, so minis are 11 pounds or less at a year of age, and most standards are more than 16 pounds. Does that mean there are no Dachsies who weigh 14 pounds? Nope, there are Dachsies who grow up to be "in between." These dogs are often available from breeders as pet puppies because they would have no future as show dogs or as breeding animals. So if size doesn't really matter to you, or if you would like a Dachsie smaller than a standard but a little sturdier than a mini, one of these in-between dogs might suit you well.

One Size Doesn't Fit All

When deciding on whether you should have a standard or a miniature (or even an "in between"), think about what you would like to do with your dog. Do you want to do some dog sports? What kind? Are you an active person who would like to take a dog along, or are you a more sedentary person? As you've seen, standards are better at some dog activities than minis and vice versa.

Do you like to snuggle and cuddle with a dog? The miniatures are the perfect size to cuddle. The standards like to cuddle, too, sometimes, and are smaller than a Labrador Retriever, but many people might find a standard (especially a bigger standard) too big for the sofa.

Think, too, about who will be living with the dog. If you have small children or are planning to start a family within the dog's lifetime, a standard is usually better with small kids. If the dog will be living only with adults, either size might suit you.

Take a good look at the characteristics of each size, taking into account that each dog is an individual, and then choose the size that would best suit you and your lifestyle.

Smooth, Longhaired, or Wirehaired?

Dachshunds come in three coat varieties: smooth, longhaired, and wirehaired. The smooth is by far the most popular, although the longhaired variety seems to be gaining in popularity. Each variety has its own description in the AKC breed standard.

Not all Dachshunds have smooth coats.

Smooth: Coat—Short, smooth and shining. Should be neither too long nor too thick. Ears not leathery. Tail—Gradually tapered to a point, well, but not too richly, haired. Long sleek bristles on the underside are considered a patch of strong-growing hair, not a fault. A brush tail is a fault, as is also a partly or wholly hairless tail.

The short, smooth coat is much like many other short-coated breeds. The shiny short coat shows of the Dachsie's physique and is by far the most recognizable coat variety. The short coat requires little grooming; a weekly brushing is usually plenty.

Longhaired: Coat—The sleek, glistening, often slightly wavy hair is longer under the neck and on the forechest, the underside of the body, the ears, and behind the legs. The coat gives the dog an elegant appearance. Short hair on the ears is not desirable. Too profuse a coat which masks type, equally long hair all over the body, a curly coat, or a pronounced parting on the back are faults. Tail—Carried gracefully in prolongation of the spine, the hair attains its greatest length here and forms a veritable flag.

This silky coat is much like the Papillon's gorgeous coat. It is soft and silky. Once you meet a longhaired Dachsie, you will find that it's hard to keep your hands off his coat! However, the longhaired Dachsie needs daily grooming. That lovely coat is, unfortunately, prone to tangles and mats. It will also pick up dirt, *burrs*, and *foxtails*.

Dog Talk

Burrs and **foxtails** are the seeds from certain grasses and weeds that easily stick to your Dachsie's coat.

Wirehaired: Coat—With the exception of the jaw, eyebrows and ears, the whole body is covered with a uniform tight, short, thick, rough, hard, outer coat but with a finer, somewhat softer, shorter hairs (undercoat) everywhere distributed between the coarser hairs. The absence of the undercoat is a fault. The distinctive facial furnishings include a beard and eyebrows. On the ears, the hair is shorter than on the body, almost smooth. The general arrangement of the hair is such that the wirehaired Dachshund, when viewed from a distance, resembles the smooth. Any sort of soft hair in the outer coat, wherever found on the body, especially on top of the head, is a fault. The same is true of long, curly, or wavy hair, or hair that sticks out irregularly in all directions. Tail—Robust, thickly haired, gradually tapering to a point. A flag tail is a fault.

The wirehaired coat is like a terrier's coat. It is tough and hardly anything gets through it. It sheds rain, and a wirehaired Dachsie can go dashing through a field of briars and come out unscathed! This is a hard coat. Show wirehaired Dachsies are hard stripped (the dead coat is pulled out to make room for new coat); however, many pet owners will have the dog clipped by a professional dog groomer.

Personality Differences?

Although most Dachsie owners and breeders stress that a Dachsie is a Dachsie, no matter what the coat variety, many others say there is a difference in personalities associated with the coat types. The smooth-coat Dachsie is said to be "the" Dachsie; the variety against which all others are judged. Owners of some longhaired Dachsies say these dogs are more cuddly than the other varieties and somewhat softer in temperament. Owners of wirehaired Dachsies say this variety is as tough as their coat; always ready for anything.

As to whether all longhaired Dachsies are cuddly or all wirehaired Dachsies are tough, well, keep in mind that each dog is an individual. I'm sure there are plenty of cuddly smooths and wirehaireds, and I've met some smooths who were pretty tough!

Choosing the Coat

Although the type of coat might not seem like a major decision, it really is. The longcoated Dachsies need regular grooming, and if that grooming isn't done, the dog could end up a matted, tangled mess. The wirehaired coat is coarse and hard. People who like terriers love this coat, but if you aren't used to it, it isn't very soft to pet.

Before you make a final decision, try to see and pet all three coat varieties. By actually petting and handling all three coats, you can decide which coat variety appeals to you.

The Many Colors of Dachshunds

Red is by far the most recognizable color of Dachshunds, although some people also recognize that Dachsies may be black with tan markings. However, did you know that Dachsies may also be the same blue merle color often seen in Australian Shepherds or Collies, or that Dachsies can be brindled like Mastiffs?

Dachshunds come in an artist's palette of colors!

The Colors

Here are a few of the colors seen in the breed:

- 🏠 **Red.** This is the most recognizable and most common color. This color is not the red of the stripes on our nation's flag, but instead is a reddish-brown. Shades vary from chestnut through brown.

- 🏠 **Wheaten.** This is a light red, and it can sometimes look faded, although that isn't desirable.

- 🏠 **Cream.** This is a cream to light beige or tan; it's not white.

🐾 **Black-and-tan.** This is the second most common Dachsie color. Many breeds have this black-and-tan pattern. The dog is black with tan marking above each eye, on the cheeks and muzzle, on the chest, under the tail, and on the legs and feet. These markings are called points.

🐾 **Chocolate-and-tan.** This color is marked just like the black-and-tan, except the parts that are black on the black-and-tan dog are chocolate (dark brown).

🐾 **Isabella-and-tan.** This color pattern is very similar to the Isabella seen in Doberman Pinschers. The base color is a gray/yellow/cream color that's very difficult to describe but unmistakable once you've seen it. Tan markings are placed just as they are on the black-and-tan and chocolate-and-tan.

___ **Dog Talk** ___

The tan markings on the black, chocolate, gray, and Isabella dogs are called **points.**

🐾 **Gray-and-tan (or blue-and-tan).** This is usually a dark gray, almost a pewter or gun metal gray. The tan markings are placed as they are with the black-and-tan.

The Color Patterns

The colors of Dachsies aren't always simple solid colors. Black-and-tan, chocolate-and-tan, and Isabella-and-tan dogs have two different colors in a set pattern. Although the extent of the tan markings may be more or less on different dogs, the placing of the markings is usually pretty uniform. But these tan markings aren't the only color patterns seen in the breed. Here are some others:

🐾 **Dappled.** The dapple pattern is like the merle color patterns found in Australian Shepherds, Collies, Shetland Sheepdogs, and some other breeds. Dapple is a lighter color over a darker color in irregular patches and splotches. The dapple pattern can be found over the other solid colors, so there may be red dapples, black-and-tan dapples, chocolate-and-tan dapples, and so forth. The eyes may be partially or entirely blue.

🏠 **Sable.** Each hair will have two colors—the base color at the base of the hair and darker (often black) color near the tip of the hair. Therefore, a red sable will have a red face and feet (where the hairs are shorter) and will look very dark over the rest of the body.

Dachsie Wisdom

In describing a Dachsie, the color is named first, then the color pattern. So a black-and-tan Dachsie with a dapple pattern is called a black-and-tan dapple.

🏠 **Wild boar.** This is found only in wirehaired Dachsies. The black coat in a black-and-tan Dachsie has an undercoat that is lighter in color.

🏠 **Double dapple.** When two dapple pattern dogs are bred together, the resulting offspring are called "double dapples." These dogs usually have more white than normal on the body, especially on the head, legs, feet, belly, and sides. Double dapples may have blue eyes.

Watch Out!

Double dapples should be bred only by breeders knowledgeable in Dachsie genetics, as they may have severe birth defects, including missing eyes, other eye defects, deafness, and more. If you're considering buying a double dapple, make sure the dog can see and hear normally. Also, get written guarantee that if the dog doesn't get a clean bill of health from your vet, you can return her.

🏠 **Brindle.** Dark stripes overlay the base color. A red brindle will have black, irregular, ragged stripes on the red base color. A black-and-tan may also be a brindle, although the stripe will only show on the tan markings because the black stripes will not show against the black base color.

🏠 **Piebald.** This is a white spotted pattern that can appear over any base color. The solid spots—which are the base color—remain true to the base color. These appear to be white dogs with patches of color, although the amount of white can vary.

> **Dachsie Wisdom**
>
> Piebald Dachsies may not be shown in any country except the United States.

Choosing a Color

Many of the possible coat colors are rarely seen. Therefore, when you're looking for a puppy, have a few color choices in mind, but don't focus on one particular color or color pattern. It would be a shame to pass up wonderful dogs of other colors just because they aren't the particular color or color pattern you're looking for.

The Least You Need to Know

🏠 The Dachshund's long back is a unique feature, but one that could cause problems.

🏠 The two sizes of Dachsies—standard and miniature—are alike, yet different.

🏠 There are three Dachsie coat varieties: smooth, longhaired, and wirehaired.

🏠 Dachsies come in a variety of colors and color patterns.

4

Finding Your Dachshund

In This Chapter

- 🏠 Finding a reputable breeder
- 🏠 Finding a Dachshund through rescue
- 🏠 Other ways to find a dog
- 🏠 Choosing the right dog for you

In previous chapters, we talked about what is needed from you as a dog owner and asked you to look at yourself, your lifestyle, and your budget to decide whether dog ownership is the right choice for you. We also discussed Dachshunds in particular and their origins, personality, temperament, and physical conformation. We looked at the differences between standard and mini Dachsies, the coat variations, and the colors found in this breed. With all those things in mind, now you need to find that particular Dachshund who will be right for you.

We'll take a look at breeders first, and explain the process of buying a dog from a breeder. You might also want to look into purebred rescue, too, as Dachshund rescue groups have many Dachsies needing homes. People also acquire dogs from other sources, including the local animal shelter, and we'll talk about the pros and cons of shelter adoptions.

This chapter will also help you choose the right puppy or dog—that unique individual—who will become your companion and best friend. Each dog is different, and choosing the right one can be tough, so we'll guide you through that process.

Finding a Reputable Breeder

The best place to find your future Dachsie soul mate is from a reputable breeder. What makes a breeder "reputable"?

- A reputable breeder is someone who loves Dachshunds enough to educate himself (or herself) about the good and not-so-good points of the breed.

- A reputable breeder recognizes that Dachshunds are not the right breed for everyone and carefully screens potential buyers so he can weed out those who wouldn't be happy with his dogs.

- A reputable breeder chooses his breeding stock carefully, using the breed standard as a guide and using health tests to try to eliminate any unhealthy dogs from the breeding program.

- Reputable breeders will supply you with proof of health screening, a sales contract, and references.

Involved in the Breed

Reputable breeders are usually quite involved in their breed. Most belong to the national breed club, the Dachshund Club of America, Inc., and many will also belong to local or regional clubs. The vast majority of reputable breeders compete in conformation dog shows so that their dogs might compete against other Dachshunds, with winners chosen by an impartial judge. Many reputable breeders are also involved with the breed's original occupation and, even if their dogs don't actually hunt, they may compete or participate in go to ground events and field trials.

Protective of Their Dogs

Reputable breeders are protective of their dogs; they don't want their dogs to end up in the wrong home, where the dog might be hurt or given up because she's the wrong dog for that owner. Therefore, a reputable breeder might ask you as many questions as you ask him. You want information about his dogs, but he wants to make sure you will be a good dog owner for one of his dogs!

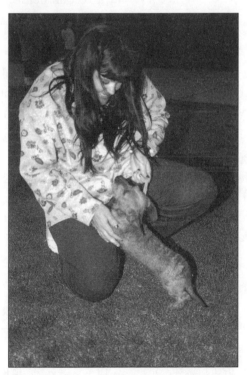

Breeders want to make sure you'll be the best owner possible for one of their puppies.

Finding That Special Breeder

There are lots of ways to find a good breeder. If someone in your neighborhood has a nice Dachsie who is healthy and has a nice personality, ask where he got his dog and whether he would recommend that breeder. Your veterinarian might also have a good breeder as a client. The American Kennel Club can give you a referral to a breeders' list or to the national club. You may also want to attend a local dog show and talk to Dachshund owners and breeders who are competing that day. Just wait until their competition is over; most will not want to talk before competing.

Dachsie Wisdom

The Dachshund Club of America, Inc., Andra O'Connell, Secretary, 1793 Berme Road, Kerhonkson, NY, 12446; www.dca.org.

Questions to Ask

Once you have a few names and numbers of potential breeders, it's time to begin making some phone calls and asking some questions. This will help you find a good reputable breeder rather than a *backyard breeder*.

My now four-year-old dog, Kes, was from a backyard breeder. I was looking for a puppy from certain lines; I knew several of the dogs in these lines and wanted a puppy who had those physical and mental characteristics. When I heard that this gentleman had puppies from these lines, I called and found that this was the first litter he had ever produced. I was concerned but decided to ask him all my questions anyway. As it turned out, even though he was a backyard breeder and this was his first litter, he had tried to do a good job and he succeeded. Kes has been a wonderful, healthy, emotionally stable dog. She has been a joy. So

Dog Talk

A **backyard breeder** is someone who has bred his dog but has done so without the knowledge the reputable breeder has. He might produce a nice litter of puppies, but it might also be a gamble.

a backyard breeder might do a super job, but he might also produce some horrible dogs. When dealing with a backyard breeder, ask the same questions you would ask a reputable breeder and be careful.

When you talk to breeders, ask them all these same questions:

- **How long have you been breeding?** Some experience is better, and my experience with Kes aside, be cautious about buying from a breeder's first litter. However, many years' experience isn't always best, either. Sometimes the "old timers" never allow themselves to learn anything new.

- **What health problems do you screen your dogs for?** If she says her dogs have no health problems, beware! Although Dachsies are quite healthy, there's no such thing as being totally health problem–free! Talk to your veterinarian, too, and find out what health problems he sees in local Dachsies.

- **What kind of guarantee do you offer with your dogs?** Is the dog or puppy guaranteed free of hereditary health defects? This is very important to you. Make sure you understand the terms of the contract. Some say that the dog must be returned to the breeder to satisfy the terms of the contract; will you be able or willing to do this?

- **Can I stop by to see some of your dogs?** The answer must be yes. You should be able to see the mother of the litter, possibly also the father. Seeing several other dogs will give you a good idea as to what the health and personality of her dogs is like.

When You First Visit the Breeder ...

When you go see the breeder the first time, there are a few things you should look for:

- Are the Dachsies happy, alert, and healthy?
- Does the breeder call each Dachsie by name?
- Is the area clean?

You should be comfortable bringing home a dog from this environment; don't try to "save" a dog from a bad breeder—that just encourages her to continue breeding!

The breeder should be able to show you registration papers for both the mother and father of the litter and litter registration papers for the litter of puppies. Her paperwork must be in order, or you won't be able to register your puppy.

You should be happy and comfortable taking home a puppy from the breeder.

The breeder should also allow you to read her sales contract. Make sure you understand the contract and are willing to agree to all parts of it.

Ask the breeder for some references, too, and follow through and call these people. Would each of these people return to this breeder for another puppy? Were they satisfied with the process of buying a puppy or dog from this breeder? If there were problems, what were they? How was the problem resolved? You can find out a lot by asking some simple questions.

The breeder will also ask you some questions; in fact, I'm always a little worried if the breeder doesn't ask me enough questions. He will want to know whether you have owned a dog before and, if you have, whether that dog lived out his life with you. If your dog was given to a shelter, was hit by a car, or died young because of negligence on your part, he's not going to be enthused about selling you one of his dogs. The breeder is also going to try and find out how much you know about Dachshunds, because he knows the breed isn't right for everyone. Don't take offense at the breeder's questions, instead, be happy he is asking them and answer them completely and truthfully.

Dachshund Rescue

Purebred dog rescue has become very active in the past decade as the population of purebred dogs being euthanized in shelters has grown. Enthusiasts of purebred dogs were horrified to find dogs of their breed being killed when potential adopters could be found. Rescue groups were formed to help save individual breeds. Some rescue groups were sponsored by national and regional breed clubs, while other groups operated independently of clubs.

There are many Dachshund rescue groups. The easiest way to find one is to search the Internet for "Dachshund rescue." Many of the rescue websites have links to other rescue groups. Some popular Dachsie rescue sites include the following:

- Coast to Coast Dachshund Rescue: www.c2cdr.org
- Dachshund Rescue of North America: www.drna.org
- Dachshund Rescue Web Page: www.drwp.net

The Rescue Process

Dachshund rescue groups work in one of two ways. Some work as referral agencies and take information about dogs needing to be given up by their owners, then refer people looking for a Dachsie to the owners of the dogs. Other groups will actually take in dogs and find foster homes for them until new adoptive owners can be found.

In both situations, you can usually find out something about the dog. Why is she being given up by her owner? Is the dog house-trained? Did the dog have any obedience training? Is the dog vaccinated and healthy?

Although you might not be able to get quite as much information about the dog's ancestors as you get from a breeder, you can usually get quite a bit of information about the dog—at least enough to decide whether the dog might be the right one for you.

> **Bet You Didn't Know**
>
> Dogs end up in rescue for horrible reasons: The dog didn't match the new carpet. The owners were moving. The dog dug a hole in the backyard. Dachsies often end up in rescue because people didn't take the time to find out what Dachsies are like!

Dachsies in Shelters

Humane societies, animal control, and other shelters often have purebred or mixed-breed Dachsies available for adoption. These dogs may have been the result of a backyard breeder who was unable to sell all her puppies or perhaps the result of an unplanned breeding. Unfortunately, Dachsies also end up in a shelter when the owner didn't do enough research on the breed and ended up with a dog he couldn't handle or didn't like.

Shelter Pros and Cons

Adopting a dog from a shelter can make you feel good; you're saving a dog who might otherwise have been euthanized. Most shelters keep dogs for a very limited period of time, and if the dog isn't adopted, he is killed. There is a real sense of pleasure in saving a life; it makes you feel good inside.

However, there is a down side to shelter adoption. The dog is usually a total unknown. A breeder can tell you a lot about individual dogs and their ancestry, and a rescue group that fosters dogs can tell you quite a bit about the dog being fostered. A shelter, however, usually has no information about the dog. You won't know where she came from, how she was treated, or even her health history.

Find Out What You Can

If you find a nice Dachsie at the local shelter, find out as much as you can before you decide whether or not to adopt this dog. Ask to see any paperwork concerning the dog. Did the person turning in the dog leave any information and if so, what?

Ask the shelter workers about the dog; how is he with people? Does he act afraid of kids? How is he with other dogs? What have they observed about his personality, behavior, and health?

Many great dogs have come from shelters, but you do have to be careful. Just find out as much as you can before you decide to bring home a shelter dog.

Dachsie Wisdom

Privacy laws may not allow the shelter to share any paperwork with you. However, if you ask, they may read you any pertinent information.

Other Ways to Find a Dog

Dogs may be acquired in many different ways. Perhaps your dentist's secretary has a Dachsie who had a litter or your neighbor's parents passed away and their Dachsie needs a home. You might see an advertisement in the pet section of the newspaper for Dachsie puppies. Or perhaps while walking past the local pet store, you see a

Dachsie puppy playing in the window. Let's take a look at some of these situations and see if they might provide you with a good Dachsie.

From Individuals

You might or might not get a good dog from a private party—an individual. There are so many factors involved that it's hard to say. I suggest you treat this the same way you would if you were buying from a breeder. Talk to the owner of the dog (when possible) or the seller of the dog and ask the same questions you would ask a breeder. If you get a bad feeling or have some reservations, don't take the dog.

> **Watch Out!**
> Don't allow yourself to "save" a Dachsie who is in a precarious position. Buying a stolen dog from an ad in the newspaper or a pet store dog will only encourage these individuals to continue their activities.

If the dog's owners have passed away, ask the person placing the dog as much as possible. What does he or she know about the dog? Keep in mind, too, that the dog may be grieving for his former owners and may not show his real personality for several weeks.

If you think you might want the dog, spend as much time with him as you can, so the dog will relax with you. Play with him, cuddle him, and take him for a walk. See if his personality shows, and notice what behavior problems he might have. Don't let the seller rush you into making a decision; that's a sure sign something is wrong!

From Pet Stores

Reputable breeders don't sell their puppies to pet stores. Reputable breeders want to know who is buying their puppies and that they are well cared for. Therefore, the sources of puppies in pet stores are usually questionable. Some may come from backyard breeders, but most come from *puppy mills*.

The Dachsies found in pet stores are as much of an unknown as are Dachsies found in shelters. Oh, the pet store puppies may come with AKC registration papers, but who knows if the papers are accurate, and the papers themselves are no assurance of quality. A pet store puppy is an unknown entity.

___ **Dog Talk** ___

Puppy mills are commercial operations that produce dogs in large numbers. Dogs are kept in cages and no screening is done as to health, temperament, or working ability prior to breeding the dogs.

Choosing the Right Dog for You

Dachshund temperaments vary considerably, so even though you might have decided that this is the right breed for you, you'll still want to find the Dachsie with a temperament that will complement your own. Choosing the wrong dog could result in years of enmity or discord. So let's look at how you can choose the best Dachsie for you.

Think About Your Own Personality

Be honest about your own personality. Are you quiet and introverted? Boisterous and extroverted? Somewhere in between? Are you bossy? Do you like to have your own way? Or do you prefer to give in so there isn't a fuss? When choosing the right dog for yourself, try to choose a dog who won't conflict with your own personality.

If you are …

- **Quiet, shy, introverted,** choose a puppy or dog who is also quiet but *don't* choose a shy dog. If both of you are shy, you'll reinforce that trait. Instead, choose a dog who is quiet but is also outgoing and self-confident.

- **Compliant,** choose a Dachsie who is calm but not bold. A bold Dachsie would take advantage of you.

- **Boisterous, bossy, and extroverted,** take the boldest puppy in the litter. You two will have a blast together.

Male or Female?

Both male and female Dachsies can be great friends and companions, but each sex does have some unique characteristics. The thing to keep in mind is that to be a good pet, neither sex needs adult sexual hormones, so the males should be neutered and females spayed. I'll be describing the characteristics of neutered males and spayed females.

Watch Out!

Male dogs, even neutered males, often lift their hind leg to urinate on upright objects to mark their territory. This can be very annoying to many people, so think about it when choosing a dog.

Neutered males are usually quite sweet. They can be rowdy and are always ready for an adventure, but usually they like to spend time with their people. Girls, even spayed girls, can be a bitch. Keep in mind, there is a reason why bitches are called bitches! Oh, the females will cuddle, too, but they can also be bossy.

As a general rule, I suggest male dog owners get a female and female dog owners get a male. There often seems to be less challenge that way. If the dog is for a family, it's a toss-up. However, male or female, always take the dog's individual personality into account.

Puppy Tests

If you have decided to get a Dachsie puppy, the following tests will help you see each puppy's individual personality traits. These tests are best done when the puppies are six to seven weeks of age. Many breeders do this themselves and could give you the results; however, if the breeder doesn't, perhaps he could help you do them.

🏠 Look at the puppies together. At six weeks of age, the puppies are interacting with each other. Who is the most aggressive puppy? Who is the most submissive? Is there a bully? The boldest puppy is usually the first to do everything and shows no fear. He might or might not be a bully. This puppy would be a good dog to do things with, especially dog sports, but might be too bold and extroverted to be a quiet house dog. The puppy who sits alone at the side away from the other puppies might be timid or fearful. Further testing might reveal whether this puppy can cope with life or whether this is a fearful puppy who doesn't want to get involved. A fearful dog is not a good one for a houseful of kids.

You can learn a lot by watching puppies interact with each other.

🏠 Set one puppy alone on the ground and, without saying anything, take a few steps away from him. If he follows you, good; this puppy should bond well to people. If he takes off on his own with nose to the ground, he should be a good field dog but may be too independent to be a "best friend."

🏠 Toss a tennis ball or crumpled piece of paper a few feet in front of the puppy. If he chases after it and brings it back to you, awesome! This puppy will be fairly receptive to training and household rules. If he chases it but doesn't bring it back, or brings it only part way back, that's okay, too. However, if the puppy ignores the ball and prefers to sniff, or if the puppy simply watches the ball roll away, this puppy could potentially be a training challenge.

🏠 Pick up the puppy and roll him over on his back in your arms. Hold him close and talk to him. Does he struggle and then stop, while looking at your face? This is fine. This puppy should accept your pack leadership. The puppy who does not stop struggling could be overly bold or dominant, while the puppy who urinates all over himself (and you) may be very fearful.

As you watch the litter of puppies, think of your own personality. Will you be able to love and tolerate (two different things!) a dog who challenges you constantly? If that would be a problem, chose a dog who follows you when you walk away, who chases after the ball and brings it back, and who settles down in your arms. However, if you yourself are bold and extroverted and you like a challenge, choose the bolder puppy. Choose the one who struggles a little more in your arms and who chases the ball but doesn't necessarily bring it back. Choose the one who tries to be the boss with his littermates.

There are no right or wrong answers here. These tests are to help you chose the right puppy for you and your family.

Testing Adult Dogs

Testing adult dogs is somewhat different than testing puppies. For one thing, their littermates aren't available, so you can't see the interaction between them. But that doesn't mean you can't see some of the dog's personality by doing some simple tests:

🏠 Take the dog to a small fenced-in yard and let him go. Just watch him. Does he sniff, relieve himself, then come over to investigate you? This dog is oriented to people. Does he sniff, look at you, then continue exploring and sniffing? This dog isn't as oriented toward people and is perhaps even standoff-ish. Does the dog cower in a corner or hide? This dog is very fearful.

🏠 Call the dog to you with a happy voice and open hands. Does he come bounding toward you? Super! Again, this dog is people-oriented and has learned that coming to people is good. Does he come to you but remain out of reach? Perhaps his former owners called him and scolded him for something. You may be able to rebuild his trust, but it will take some work and lots of patience. If he ignores you or runs the other way, this dog could be a challenge.

> **Watch Out!**
>
> If you have kids or grandkids, don't take home a dog who wants to chase and possibly bite children!

🏠 Without risking other dogs or people, observe the dog's reaction to children, senior adults, and other dogs. Is the dog reacting in a way that you would be comfortable dealing with? Training can solve some problems, but it takes time so make sure the dog doesn't have any socialization problems you aren't prepared to deal with.

Listen to Your Heart

Choosing the right puppy or dog can be hard. An emotional decision is rarely the right one, yet the decision can't be made totally without emotion, either. The tests in this chapter are a tool to help you choose the right puppy or dog for you. However, to choose the right Dachshund for you, you must also be honest about yourself. Finally, make sure you like each other. After all, that's what is most important.

The Least You Need to Know

🏠 A reputable breeder will be able to tell you all about her dogs' ancestors. Ask her lots of questions and expect to answer her questions.

🏠 Adopting a dog from Dachshund rescue is a possibility, although you probably won't know as much about the dog as you would from a breeder.

🏠 Adopting a dog from a shelter will save the dog's life, but you probably won't know anything about him.

🏠 Behavior testing can help you choose the right puppy or dog for you.

Part 2

There's a Puppy in the House!

A new dog is the future waiting to happen. There's so much you and this dog can do together—so much to see, hear, explore, and share. You need to be prepared for this new member of the family. You'll need to go shopping for dog food, bowls, a crate, a leash, and a collar. Oh, and how about dog toys? You'll also need to dog-proof your house and yard so your Dachsie will be safe.

What next? How about setting some rules? When your Dachsie is full grown, how do you want him to behave in the house? This is when you need to start introducing some household rules. You also need to begin housetraining your Dachsie and socializing him to the world around him.

There's a lot to know, so keep reading!

Good dog!

Chapter 5

Prior Planning Prevents Chaos!

In This Chapter

- 🏠 Shopping for supplies
- 🏠 Making your house safe
- 🏠 Making your yard safe
- 🏠 How pet professionals can help
- 🏠 Other necessary items

So you are going to bring home a Dachshund. Your life will never again be the same! But don't worry, the change is definitely for the better.

Before you bring home your new best friend, though, there are some preparations you'll need to do.

First of all, you'll need to go shopping. You'll need dog food, food and water bowls, a leash and collar, and some other essentials. You'll also need to make sure your house is safe for your new dog.

Fragile knick-knacks will need to be put away, slippers and shoes put back in closets, and electrical cords tucked out of sight and reach. The backyard will also need to be made Dachshund escape-proof and safe.

You'll also want to have some pet professionals lined up to help you. A veterinarian is your partner in your Dachshund's good health, and a trainer can help you teach your Dachsie good manners. If you have a longhaired or wirehaired Dachsie, a groomer can help you with that coat.

Let's Go Shopping!

If you already have a dog at home you may have some of the basic supplies your new Dachsie will need. However, if this is your first dog, you'll need to go shopping. The things listed here are the basics; you may want to buy additional things later, but right now we'll begin with only the necessities.

Your Dachsie will need some essential supplies.

Dog Food

Find out from the breeder or former owner of the dog what he's been feeding your new Dachsie. Make sure you have at least a two-week supply of that food on hand. If for some reason you or your veterinarian want to change foods, that's okay, just do so gradually over two weeks. If you change foods suddenly, your new dog will suffer from gastrointestinal upset—often diarrhea.

Food and Water Bowls

You'll want to have two solid, heavy bowls that won't tip over. Dachsies are known for playing with their bowls, and you don't want a water bowl (especially a full one!) to become a play toy!

Dachsie Wisdom

Ceramic bowls can break and plastic bowls may get chewed up, so invest in metal bowls from the beginning.

Collar and Leash

A soft nylon buckle collar is fine to start, with a four-foot-long matching (if you wish!) nylon leash. You might need other collars later for training, but this will get you started.

Identification

You'll want to put some identification on your new Dachsie right away. Most pet stores have machines that will make engraved tags while you wait. Make sure the tag has all of your phone numbers on it. Put this tag on your Dachsie's collar.

Later, you can talk to your veterinarian about having a microchip injected under the skin at your Dachsie's shoulder. This is a permanent identification and is recommended by most pet professionals.

Crate

A crate is a wonderful training tool for your Dachsie. In future chapters, you'll learn how to introduce your Dachsie to the crate and how to use it for housetraining and problem prevention. For now, just remember that the crate should be large enough for your Dachsie to lie down, turn around, and be comfortable.

When you shop for the crate, you'll find they come in two basic types. The plastic ones are the kind used by airlines to ship animals; in fact, on televised animal shows you will see zoo animals and wildlife transported in these. These are solid sided and provide shelter and security. There are also wire crates with barred sides. These provide more air flow and in hot climates might work better for your Dachsie. Look at both types of crates and chose the one that will serve you best.

Baby Gates

Baby gates were designed to keep human toddlers in (or out of) certain rooms or restricted to certain areas to keep them out of trouble. Baby gates are also wonderful for puppies, as they can serve the same purpose. Get as many as you need to keep your Dachsie out of trouble.

Bet You Didn't Know

Garage sales are a great place to pick up baby gates at a very cheap price.

Grooming Supplies

The type of grooming supplies you need will depend on the type of coat your Dachsie has. For example, a smooth Dachsie will need a soft-bristle brush, toenail clippers, and shampoo. A longcoated Dachsie will also need a comb and a dematter brush. Talk to your new dog's breeder or a groomer about the supplies you'll need. You don't have to go overboard and buy everything right now, just get the basics—what you need to care for your Dachsie now.

Cleaning Supplies

You'll want to have some white vinegar on hand to clean up after housetraining accidents. (Don't use ammonia cleaners, because they smell like urine to your Dachsie.) Paper towels, a scrub brush, and trash bags will be all you'll need—at least in the beginning.

Toys

Your Dachsie will need toys to play with and chew on, so wander down the toy aisle at the local pet store and choose a few sturdy toys. Make sure the toy can't be destroyed by strong Dachshund teeth and jaws. My dogs like Kong toys. These are hard, rubber, hollow toys. When thrown, they bounce irregularly and are fun to chase. Plus, the hollow middle can be filled with soft cheese or peanut butter and can occupy an otherwise bored dog. The toys that dispense treats are also good for occupying your dog when you're busy.

> **Bet You Didn't Know**
> Having too many toys is not better. If your Dachsie has many toys, he might think the whole world is his to chew on and destroy. Instead, just give him two or three toys at a time.

Toys are a necessity, of course!

Making Your House Safe

Your Dachsie will need to learn household rules, and that includes what is his to chew on and what isn't. While he's learning that, you need to make sure your house is safe for him. Figure out what rooms he will spend time in while learning household rules. He should not have free run of the house—not now and not until he's full-grown and well trained. So you only need to make safe the rooms he will spend time in.

 Dachsie Wisdom
Dachsie puppies are called carpet sharks for a reason: Everything goes in their mouth. So pick up and put away everything!

 **Watch Out!**
If you think your Dachsie has chewed or eaten something dangerous, call the National Poison Control Hotline at 1-800-222-1222 or APSCA Animal Poison Control at 1-888-426-4435.

In those rooms, pick up knick-knacks, put away books and magazines, and close closet doors. Put away or pick up anything that can be chewed or destroyed. Tuck away electrical and telephone cords. Make sure the television remote control is out of reach.

From Your Dachsie's Point of View

To make sure your house is safe, you must get down on your hands and knees and look at your house from your Dachsie's point of view. It's the only way to see what he sees. After all, your point of view is from above; his is much, much lower.

So get down on your hands and knees and look around. That telephone cord dangling off the end table is very inviting; a puppy will chew on that and probably pull the phone off the table. Those magazines under the end table will be shredded, so pick them up. The VCR tapes on the shelf under the VCR will be played with and perhaps chewed on.

Make sure everyone in the family understands the new rules. If someone leaves his or her slippers in the room with the new dog and he chews them up, it's not the dog's fault! He doesn't know any better until he's been taught the rules.

Dangerous Stuff

Our homes are full of things that are dangerous to our dogs. Make sure all these things are put away and safely out of an inquisitive dog's reach.

Some dangerous stuff …

- **In the kitchen:** oven cleaners, floor cleaners, wax, bug spray and insect traps, furniture polish, and dishwasher soaps and rinses

- **In the bathroom:** medicines, vitamins, bathroom cleaners, toilet bowl cleaners, some shampoos and conditioners, hair coloring products, and makeup items

- **In the rest of the house:** cigarettes, pens and felt-tip pens, many houseplants, laundry products, and craft products

- **In the garage:** car maintenance products, including oils, gas, and antifreeze; fertilizers, weed and insect control products, snail and slug bait; mouse and rat traps and poisons; and paints and paint removers

> **Watch Out!**
> Don't assume your Dachsie will not touch dangerous items. Instead, assume he will and make sure they're out of reach.

Protect Your Dachsie

Protect your Dachsie by making sure everything potentially dangerous is picked up and put away out of reach. Limit your Dachsie's freedom by using his crate to confine him when you can't supervise him and by using baby gates to limit his access to certain rooms in the house. Then, as he grows up, matures mentally, and learns the household rules, you can allow him more freedom.

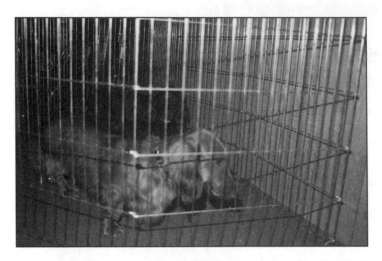

Keeping your dog safe means he will be around longer for you to love and for him to love you.

Making Your Yard Safe

You'll want to patrol your yard looking for dangerous things just like you did in the house. Pick up the kids' toys, put away your gardening gloves, and make sure fertilizers and weed control products are out of reach. Just as you did in the house, assume that something left within reach can be chewed up.

Protect Your Garden

If you have a special garden, fence it off so your new dog can't get into it. If you don't, he will be sure to dig up that good-smelling compost or will bury a favorite toy at the base of your favorite rose bush. If he has access, he may also decide to help himself to the strawberries as they ripen. So put up a decorative but sturdy fence and protect your garden.

Some Plants Are Dangerous

Many common landscaping plants are dangerous. Some will just make a dog mildly ill, but some are very toxic. Before allowing your dog free access to the yard, make sure none of these plants are present. This is a list of many of the most common poisonous plants; however, if you have any doubts about a plant's safety, talk to a horticulturist or a poison control center.

Amaryllis	Hemlock
Avocado (leaves, not fruit)	Horse chestnut
Azalea	Hyacinth
Belladonna	Iris
Bird of paradise	Jasmine
Bottlebrush	Lily of the valley
Boxwood	Milkweed
Buttercup	Morning glory
Calla lily	Mushrooms
Common privet	Oleander
Crocus	Pennyroyal
Daffodil	Poison ivy, oak, and sumac
Dieffenbachia	Rhododendron
Dogwood	Sweet pea
English ivy	Tulip
Foxglove	Yew

Make Your Fence Escape-Proof

Dachshunds are escape artists. They don't necessarily want to go anywhere; they're just curious. They also don't realize that the fence keeps them safe. So when there is a loose board on the fence, or a small gap under it, Dachsies will work at that weakness until they can get through or under the fence.

Inspect the entire fence. Pull on each board or section of the fence to make sure it's secure and tight. Replace broken boards and shore up weaknesses. You may even want to fasten wire fencing to the inside of the fence to reinforce it.

Make sure there are no gaps under the fence, too. Use big rocks, concrete blocks, or wire fencing to block any potential escape routes.

Nothing Wrong with a Dog Run

If you have some doubts about making your yard safe, keeping the dog out of the garden, or making your fence escape-proof, build your Dachsie a dog run. The dog run doesn't have to be huge—12 feet by 4 feet is more than enough. A secure, safe dog run is a much better solution than chaining your dog (which results in problem behaviors) and is safer than an inadequate fence.

Just make sure the dog run always has some shade, has unspillable water, and your dog gets lots of time outside of the dog run with you when you can supervise him.

Pet Professionals Can Help You

Pet professionals can help you immensely with your Dachsie. A groomer can help you trim those toenails the first time or show you how to strip your wirehair's coat. A trainer can give you housetraining advice and show you how to teach your Dachsie to come when called. The veterinarian should be your partner in your dog's continued good health and, of course, should be available for emergencies.

Watch Out!
Don't wait until there is an emergency to find pet professionals. Do it now before you need their help.

You can find pet professionals in several ways, but usually the best way is by personal referrals. If you ask several dog owners which veterinarian they recommend and one vet's name keeps popping up, he or she is probably a good choice.

Yellow Page ads are fine, but anyone can advertise. People who have had experience with certain professionals, however, can tell you the good and bad points of those professionals.

Introduce Yourself

When you have referrals to several pet professionals, call and make an appointment to meet each one. Introduce yourself, tell them when you are bringing your Dachsie home, and ask them about themselves and their business. What are their business hours? What are their payment procedures? Do they accept credit cards? What are their emergency policies? Are they ever available after hours?

Ask your vet if he has any specialties, such as allergies or internal medicine. Ask what he thinks about Dachshunds and their health and whether he is familiar with Dachshund back problems. Ask about his payment policies for emergencies.

The trainer should also be familiar with Dachshunds and knowledgeable of their training needs. The groomer should know how to groom a wirehair's coat, or know what tools work best on the longhair's coat.

When you have talked to several veterinarians, trainers, and groomers, you should have a good idea as to whom you will feel better doing business with. Set up a client record with each before your dog comes home. This way, if you have a problem, you have someone available to call when you need it.

What Else Do You Need?

How about a couple old towels for your Dachsie's crate? Don't buy an expensive dog bed right now; it would just get chewed up. You can buy one later when your Dachsie is grown up and would appreciate it.

How about a long leash or a length of clothesline rope to take your dog out to play? You don't want to let him off leash until he's full grown, mentally mature, and well trained, but meanwhile, a long leash will give him a chance to play when you go to the park.

That should do it. Now you're ready to bring home your Dachshund!

The Least You Need to Know

- 🏠 You need to do some shopping before you bring home your Dachshund. Get dog food, bowls, a leash and collar, a crate, and some toys.

- 🏠 Make your home safe for your dog, and don't forget to look at things from your Dachsie's eye level as you do so.

- 🏠 Make sure your fence is escape-proof and your yard is safe.

- 🏠 Find a veterinarian and other pet professionals so you will have some help should you need it.

Chapter 6

Is It Your House or Your Dachshund's House?

In This Chapter

- 🏠 The importance of rules
- 🏠 Deciding what those rules will be
- 🏠 Preventing problems before they start
- 🏠 How to be your Dachshund's leader

It doesn't matter whether you have brought home a Dachshund puppy or adult, it's never too early to start teaching your dog some household rules. By beginning his instruction right away, he will never learn the unacceptable behaviors that so many puppies do learn: the behavior that often results in the dog being exiled to the backyard. Teach him as a young dog what is expected of him, and he will grow up that way.

If you have brought home an adult Dachshund, the same thing applies. Your home is a new start for him. If he had bad behaviors in his former home, don't let them continue in your home.

It's Your House; You Can Set Some Rules

Because your Dachsie is joining you in your house (not you in his!), you have every right to set some rules of acceptable behavior in the house. After all, you're paying the bills, buying the dog food, and cleaning up all the messes. You have every right to expect a certain level of behavior.

When you establish these rules very early—as soon as the Dachsie joins your family—your dog never learns the wrong behavior. For example, if you want the Dachshund to stay off the furniture, never allow him up on the furniture. Some dog owners will allow the puppy up when he's a baby and then when the dog is an adolescent and is bouncing off the back of the sofa, they want to change the rules and keep the dog on the floor. That's not fair! Instead, start teaching the Dachsie now, when he first joins your household, exactly what you expect of him. He's capable of learning; you just need to teach him.

Dachsie Wisdom

By 8 to 10 weeks of age, the Dachsie's brain is fully functional and capable of incredible learning. All we need to do is teach him!

Be Consistent

When you establish the household rules, make sure everyone in the household will accept them and enforce them. If your teenage son likes to cuddle with the Dachsie on the sofa and encourages the dog to get up there whenever no one will see them, your dog will be confused. Is he supposed to get up there or not? In addition, whenever anyone else catches him up there the Dachsie will be corrected. This encouragement from one person and correction from everyone else is very confusing and entirely unfair to the dog. Everyone must be consistent with the rules.

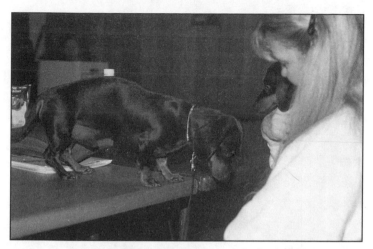

Do you want your Dachshund on the furniture?

Posting a list of the rules in a prominent location works for many Dachsie owners. List a command, such as "Off the sofa!" so that everyone is using the same language. Put the list on the refrigerator where everyone will see it on a daily basis.

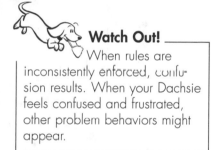

Watch Out!
When rules are inconsistently enforced, confusion results. When your Dachsie feels confused and frustrated, other problem behaviors might appear.

What Will the Rules Be?

When trying to decide what rules you would like to establish, keep in mind what your dog will grow up to be. Both standard and miniature Dachshunds are relatively small dogs, but standards can take up some room on the sofa. Do you want him up there? Plus, Dachsies are active, so think about what effect that will have on your furniture. I like to cuddle with my dogs, so they are invited up on the furniture but they are not allowed to play on the furniture.

Your rules should also take into account your daily routine. A dog will change your routine, especially if you haven't had a dog before, but you can work a compromise between your normal routine before-dog and after-dog.

A dog underfoot in the kitchen can be a hazard.

Some Suggestions

Following are a few suggestions for some relatively easy to teach household rules:

🏠 Do you want to allow the Dachsie in the kitchen? Some dog owners like to keep the dog in the kitchen because if he has an accident there, it's easy to clean up. I don't like to allow my dogs in the kitchen because there are too many dangers there

for my peace of mind. I don't want the dogs underfoot when
I'm cooking or using a sharp knife. There are cleansers and
other dangerous substances under the kitchen sink. So I teach
my puppies to stay out of the kitchen. You can weigh the pros
and cons and decide for yourself if the Dachsie allowed in the
kitchen or not.

Is the Dachsie allowed up on the furniture? The downfall of
allowing the dogs on the furniture is the added wear and tear,
the dirt, and the dog hair. I compensate for some of that by
keeping a blanket or sheet over the sofa to protect it.

Is the Dachsie to be allowed up on your bed or up on the kids'
beds? Many dog owners like to let their dog sleep on their bed.
However, this is one household rule that I feel pretty strongly
about: The dog should not be allowed to sleep on your bed!
He should sleep in your room but in his crate or in his own bed.
If you happen to have a dog with a more dominant personality
(as is so common with Dachsies!), sleeping with you will give
him delusions of grandeur! He will think he's just as good as
you are because he also sleeps in the big bed! He shouldn't
sleep in your bed or your kids' beds; he needs his own.

Watch Out! _____

If your dog is already sleeping on the bed and growls at you
when you move or ask him to get off the bed, call a dog
trainer or behaviorist for help right away. This can be a serious behavior problem that has been known to end up with the
dog biting the owner.

Is the Dachsie to be allowed to beg for food while you're eating? This isn't an acceptable habit, either. The dog who begs
for food usually ends up being a big pest, pawing legs, licking
hands, or even stealing food. If you don't want to allow begging, make sure no one feeds the Dachsie as they eat.

🏠 Do you want to restrict certain parts of the house? If you want to keep the dog out of the kids' rooms so he won't get into their stuff, that's fine. If you have a nice formal living room, teach him to stay in the family room and restrict him from the living room. In fact, as I've mentioned before, the Dachsie *does not* and *should not* have free run of the house. To restrict his access, close doors and use baby gates to keep him in the rooms where he is allowed.

🏠 Housetraining is an obvious rule, but you would be surprised at the number of dogs who aren't well housetrained. You should want your Dachsie to understand where he is allowed to relieve himself and where he should not.

🏠 Inappropriate chewing is another rule that all dogs should understand. Dog toys are for chewing; furniture, kids' toys, shoes, and other personal items are not.

What else is important to you? Think about it. What will make life with a dog easier?

Prevention Is the Best Cure!

It's always easier to teach the Dachsie what you want him to know instead of breaking or correcting a bad habit later. By preventing problems from occurring in the first place, you can teach your Dachsie acceptable behavior. If your dog learns bad behavior and thinks it's fun, changing it later can be very difficult.

For example, if your dog never learns the joys of chewing a hole in a sofa throw pillow—shaking stuffing all over—you will be able to trust him in the house alone much sooner than you will a dog who likes the fun of chewing up stuff. By preventing bad behavior, you can make your training much, much easier.

Restrict Access

Part of preventing bad behavior is restricting your Dachsie's access. Keep him in the room with you, and keep an eye on him. Don't allow him to sneak off down the hallway where he can get into trouble without you knowing about it.

Teach Him

You also need to teach your Dachsie what is acceptable and what is not. When he grabs the sofa throw pillow, take it away from him and hand him one of his toys instead. When he picks up your good leather shoes, take them away, put them in the closet, close the closet door, and hand the Dachsie one of his toys.

I made a mistake years ago and allowed one of my dogs too much freedom too soon, and she found out that trash cans had food in them. Because she was very food-motivated, this made a big impression on her and she never, ever forgot it. I learned my lesson, though, and with my next dog, I made sure her access was restricted and her freedom curtailed until she was old enough to be trusted. Now Dax, as an adult, can be trusted totally in the house. I can even leave food on the coffee table and it will still be there when I come home. Riker, my youngest dog, is being trained the same way. Although it will be a while before he is trustworthy in the house alone, he is learning and I am preventing him from learning those potentially bad habits.

Preventing problems from happening may take some work on your part. You'll have to look at your house and yard from your Dachsie's perspective: What is attractive to your Dachsie? Can he reach your potted plants? The hose is fun to chew on—can you put it out of his reach? What about the outside trash cans—are they where he can get into them?

Dachsie Wisdom

When your Dachsie is doing something right, give him permission to do it and praise him. For example, if he picks up his toy instead of your shoe, tell him, "Get your toy! Good boy!" Reinforce that good behavior!

Don't allow your Dachsie the joy of discovering what a trash can is!

Be Your Dachsie's Leader

When your Dachsie was still with his mother, she started teaching him. He followed her out to the yard, watched where she relieved herself, then did as she did. He watched her play with a toy, then tried to play with her. She was teaching him what it was like to be a dog.

Well, now it's your turn to continue her teaching. Your Dachsie needs a *leader.* The leader is fair, never asking anything that the Dachsie is unable to give. Corrections, commands, and praise will be given as needed, again in a spirit of fairness. The leader is firm when needed but is always affectionate and loving. The leader always demands respect.

> **Dog Talk**
>
> The **leader** is always fair but firm and demands respect.

If you aren't your Dachsie's leader, you won't be respected. From the dog's perspective, a dog who is not respected is considered weak and the lowest of the low. The one who isn't respected is dominated; often by mounting behavior. The low dog on the totem pole has his food stolen from him, gets no toys, and is often growled at, snapped at, and otherwise tormented. That should not and cannot be your position in your dog's pack!

Friendship Comes Later

Some dog owners want to be their dog's buddy and best friend. That's usually possible; after all, that's why we have dogs! However, it's usually possible later; after the dog is grown up and mature. During puppyhood, you must be your dog's leader, not his equal or best buddy. He must learn to respect you as well as love you.

Establish Leadership

Here are a few things you can do to help your Dachsie understand your leadership. They aren't necessarily the things his mother would do—after all we aren't dogs—but they are things you can do that will help your Dachsie understand your respective places in the family pack.

- 🏠 You should always eat first; then feed your Dachsie. In a wild pack—which we know is not the same as our family but serves as a good example—the leaders of the pack always eat first and best. Then the subordinate pack members eat. To your dog, you should be the giver of the food. This makes you very important. To maximize this importance, you should eat breakfast or dinner first, then give your Dachsie his meal.

- 🏠 You should go through doors first; then give permission for your Dachsie to either stay behind or to follow you. The Dachsie who dashes through doorways is going to get into trouble. One day he may dash out the front door ahead of you and end up in the street in front of a car. Or he may trip you, causing you to fall. You have the right to tell him to wait for your permission.

🏠 Each and every day, have your Dachsie lie down and roll over for a tummy rub. This is a submissive position, and even though he probably loves the tummy rub, it is still a position that is showing him to be submissive to you. This is good! As the leader, you have to be more dominant than he is.

🏠 Each and every day, at least once, bend over and hug your Dachsie to your knees. Don't kneel down to his level, but instead, bend over him, hugging him close as you pet him and praise him. This is a dominant position. Again, that's good.

🏠 When you pick up your Dachsie, hold him under your arm, not against your chest so that his head is up near yours. That is elevating him to a more dominant position.

🏠 Give him permission to do things. If he's picking up his ball, tell him to get his ball and then praise him for doing it. This is what some trainers call "free" training. The Dachsie was going to do it anyway, so take advantage of it!

Watch Out!

If you have an adult dominant dog, don't try these exercises without consulting a dog trainer or behaviorist first. These exercises are for puppies, and an adult dog could take offense, especially if the dog doesn't view you as his leader.

The Least You Need to Know

🏠 It's your house, so set some rules of behavior that will make life with the dog easier.

🏠 In making those rules, remember to think about what your dog will be like as an adult. Do you want an active dog bouncing on your furniture?

🏠 Preventing problems from happening is a huge part of teaching the Dachsie household rules.

🏠 You must be your Dachsie's leader—after all, you pay the bills!

Chapter 7

There Is No Such Thing as an Accident!

In This Chapter

- 🏠 Housetraining your Dachsie
- 🏠 Setting a routine and sticking to it
- 🏠 Introducing your Dachsie to his crate
- 🏠 When accidents happen …

When housetraining your Dachshund, what do you want him to understand? Most Dachsie owners want to teach their dog to relieve himself outside, sometimes in a particular area, and they want the Dachsie to be able to tell them when he needs to go outside.

It's also very helpful to teach your dog a command that means "Try to go now," so when you're taking your Dachsie for a walk, when you're letting him out in bad weather or when you're traveling, he will at least try to relieve himself when you ask him to.

Housetraining doesn't have to be horrible, although many dogs and owners have a hard time doing it. Housetraining takes consistency, repetition, and lots of patience.

How Can a Crate Help?

Adding a Dachshund to the household can be a wonderful experience, but that wonder will disappear quickly if the carpets are being ruined by housetraining accidents. However, there is a training tool that will enable you to train your new companion and avoid disaster: a crate. A crate (often called a kennel or a kennel crate) is a travel carrier for dogs. Originally used for dogs being transported on airplanes, they are now used to help dogs learn housetraining skills.

All dogs are born with the instinct to keep their beds clean. When your Dachsie was old enough and strong enough to toddle away from his brothers and sisters, he would do so to relieve himself. Before that, his mother stimulated him to relieve himself and cleaned up after him. Using a crate as a training tool takes advantage of your Dachsie's instincts to keep his bed clean to help him develop more bladder and bowel control. It also helps him learn that there are right and wrong places to relieve himself.

> **Watch Out!**
> Often puppies purchased from a pet store are difficult to housetrain. In a pet store, a puppy has to relieve himself in his cage; he has no other choice. A crate doesn't work for many of these puppies because they lose their inhibition to soil their bed.

A crate can be a wonderful training tool to help teach housetraining skills.

Two Types of Crates

There are two types of crates available. The first type is made of plastic or fiberglass. It has a metal barred door and barred windows for ventilation on each side. These come in two parts, top and bottom, and are easily cleaned. This type of crate is bulky but fairly light-weight.

Heavy-gauge wire crates are more like a cage. These usually have a metal tray in the bottom that can be pulled out to be cleaned. These crates can often be folded down to make a flat package for storage, but they are very heavy.

Which kind to use is personal preference. I think the plastic crates provide your Dachsie with more security, but the metal ones provide more ventilation. Look at the different types in the local pet supply store and choose the type will suit your needs best.

Not a Jail

It's important that you, as the new Dachsie owner, understand that the crate is not a jail. A crate is your Dachsie's own personal space; it is his den or cave. It is a place where he can hide his favorite toys or bones. He can retreat to his crate when he's tired or doesn't feel good. He will sleep in his crate at night and will spend some time there during the day when you're unable to supervise him.

Choose a crate that will allow your Dachsie to stand up, turn around, and stretch out, but don't get one that would fit a German Shepherd. Too much room isn't better. If the crate is too big, your Dachsie can relieve himself in a back corner and still have room to get away from it. The purpose of using a crate to house-train your Dachsie is to utilize his instinct to keep his bed clean.

> **Bet You Didn't Know**
>
> Puppies like to sleep in small, close places. That's why a Dachsie will curl up under the coffee table or under the foot of your recliner. A crate enables you to use this instinct as a training tool.

Introducing the Crate

Hopefully, your Dachsie's breeder has introduced your Dachsie to a crate. However, if she didn't or if you got your Dachsie from somewhere else, you'll need to introduce him to the crate. Take your time doing this; you want your Dachsie to be comfortable with the crate.

Open the door to the crate and toss a treat inside. Tell him, "Sweetie, go to bed!" as you urge your dog toward the crate. Let him go in, grab the treat, and come back out. Repeat this a few times until he seems comfortable with the crate.

Now start feeding your dog in the crate, again with the door wide open. Set the food in the back of the crate. Feed the next couple meals like this, with the door open. When your Dachsie is going all the way inside to eat with no signs of stress, close the door behind him. Do *not* let him out if he throws a fit! You don't want him to learn that barking, crying, and screaming will cause you to let him out. Instead, let him out when he's finished his meal and is calm.

Dachsie Wisdom

Dachshunds are not dumb! If they figure out that screaming will get you to open the crate door, they'll do it! Don't let your Dachshund train you!

Put the crate in your bedroom at night so your Dachsie can hear you, smell you, and be close to you all night. This is eight hours of closeness that you couldn't find the time for at any other time of day. With your Dachsie close to you, you can hear him if he gets restless and needs to go outside. If he doesn't have to go outside and is just restless, you can reach over, tap the top of the crate and tell him, "No! Quiet!"

During the day, put your Dachsie in his crate for a few minutes here and there—whenever you are too busy to supervise him. Because he has to spend many hours in his crate at night, try to limit his time in it during the day to short time periods. Twenty minutes here and thirty minutes there are okay as long as he gets plenty of attention, exercise, and time with you in between times in the crate.

The crate should *not* be used to confine your dog all day. If you and other family members work all day, arrangements must be made so that your Dachsie has a safe place to stay during the day. He cannot be kept in his crate all day long every day. Instead, build him a safe place in the backyard, such as a dog run, where he has shade, toys to play with, fresh, unspillable water, and a few snacks. Maybe even turn a radio on to easy listening music. Ask a neighbor to come over during the day to play with your Dachsie so he isn't alone all day.

Preventing Problems

The kennel crate can help you prevent problems from happening. As mentioned in Chapter 6, if you can prevent your Dachsie from learning bad habits, training will be much easier. In addition, damage caused by your dog will be much less and stress will be reduced—yours and your Dachsie's!

When you can't supervise your dog, put him outside in a safe place in the yard (his dog run if you have one) or put him in his crate. By ensuring he doesn't get into trouble, you are preventing problem behavior. He will never learn that it's fun to chew up the sofa cushions if he never gets a chance to do it! By preventing the bad behavior, you can also ensure the dog learns good habits. For example, your dog learns to chew on the toys you give him rather than learning to be destructive.

There's No Place Like Home!

Once your Dachshund is comfortable with the crate, it becomes a place of security. You can then bring the crate with you in the car, strapped down with seat belts, so that the dog is secure and safe. You can also take the crate when you travel, and the dog will always have his bed from home no matter where you go. Your dog is safe, is protected from danger, and is kept from getting into trouble.

As an Adult

As your dog grows up (in two or more years) you can give him more freedom, but you will find he will still want his crate. The crate is his bed and place of refuge, and although he may choose to sleep elsewhere once in a while, he will always want his crate available.

Housetraining Your Dachsie

Neither housetraining nor housebreaking seem to be the right words for what we're talking about. We want to teach your Dachsie to relieve himself outside—not in the house—and to try to go when we tell him to.

Take your Dachsie outside to relieve himself and go out with him.

With all the conflicting advice and misinformation about housetraining bombarding new Dachsie owners, it's amazing that so many
dogs do eventually become well housetrained. Housetraining doesn't
have to be mysterious or confus-
ing. If you understand your
Dachsie's need to keep his bed
clean, limit your Dachsie's freedom, teach him what you want
and where you want it, and set a
good schedule, your Dachsie will
cooperate.

Watch Out!
Don't teach your
Dachsie to relieve himself on
newspaper on the floor unless
you actually want him to go
potty in the house, on newspaper. Instead, start taking him
outside right away.

Good Teaching!

Take your Dachsie outside where you want him to relieve himself.
Stand outside with him, but don't interact with him. When your
Dachsie starts to sniff and circle, just watch. After he has started to
relieve himself, tell him softly, "Go potty! Good boy to go potty!"
(Using, of course, whatever vocabulary you wish to use.) When he
has completed his business, praise him even more.

You will need to go out with him to this particular spot every
time he needs to go for several weeks. Yes, weeks! That means taking him out six to eight times a day for weeks. You cannot simply
send your Dachsie outside. If you do, how do you know he has done
what he needs to do? How can you teach him the command if you
aren't there? And how can you praise him for doing what needs to
be done if you aren't there?

Housetraining is a very important skill, and many dogs end up at
animal control shelters all over the country because they haven't
been well housetrained. Take your time right now and teach this
correctly; it's too important to take lightly.

Establishing a Schedule

Housetraining is much easier if your Dachsie eats, sleeps, and goes outside on a fairly regular schedule. Variations are allowed, of course, but not too many.

Keep in mind that a young Dachsie will need to eat two to three times per day. He will need to go outside to relieve himself after each meal. He will also need to go outside after playing, when waking up from a nap, and about every two hours in between.

As he gets older and develops more bladder and bowel control, he will be able to go longer between trips outside, but this is a gradual process. Many puppies can be considered housetrained and reliable by five to six months of age as long as they are not required to hold it too long. However, it is not unusual for some puppies to need a strict schedule and many trips outside until six, seven, and even eight months of age. Just as some children potty train at different ages and rates, so do puppies. A Dachsie is housetrained and reliable when he is ready and able to do it.

Dachsie Wisdom

Tiny miniature Dachsies often seem to have more difficulty with housetraining than their larger cousins. Some experts feel the size of the world around them is a problem. Others feel a tiny bladder makes it harder. In any case, some of the minis need more help. Make sure they get outside regularly.

When Accidents Happen

Accidents will happen, but housetraining accidents happen for a reason; they aren't true "accidents." Housetraining accidents happen when the dog wasn't supervised closely enough, or the dog was given too much freedom too soon. Accidents are usually the dog owner's mistake, not the dog's!

Perhaps you won't be watching your Dachsie close enough and he will urinate on the floor. When an accident does happen, you must handle it very carefully. It is important your Dachsie learns that urinating and defecating are not wrong, but the place where he did it was wrong. If your Dachsie feels that relieving himself is wrong, he will become sneaky about it and you will find puddles in strange places behind the furniture.

If you come upon your Dachsie as he is having an accident, use a verbal correction: "Acck! What are you doing?" Scoop him up and take him outside. Then clean up the mess, but don't let him watch you clean it up. If you find an accident after the fact, do not correct your Dachsie—it's too late.

Don't rub your Dachsie's nose in his mess—that teaches him that the urine or defecation causes the problem and that's not what you want him to learn. Don't drag him to his mess and shake him or yell at him; that will only confuse him. Remember, the act of relieving himself isn't wrong; it is the act of relieving himself in the house that is wrong. Make sure your message is very clear.

When Too Many Accidents Happen

If your Dachsie is having a few accidents in the house, you need to make sure you are going outside with him so you can praise him when he relieves himself outside. Make sure he knows when and where it is right. You will also need to pay more attention to your Dachsie's schedule; are you getting him outside enough and at the right times? You also might be letting him have too much freedom; limit his access to the house so that he can't go sneaking off to another room.

Successful housetraining is based on setting your Dachsie up for success by allowing few accidents to happen and always praising your Dachsie when he relieves himself outside.

Using the "Go Potty!" Command

It's important that your Dachsie understands his command to relieve himself. If you take your Dachsie to go visit someone, it is very nice to be able to tell the dog to relieve himself before going inside the house. The same thing works when you're traveling. If you stop to get gas, you can then tell the dog to try to relieve himself, and even if his bladder isn't full, he can try.

Start using a command when you first start housetraining your Dachsie. Tell him "Go potty!" (using the vocabulary that is comfortable to you), and praise him when he does relieve himself. "Good boy to go potty!"

As his housetraining gets better and more reliable, use the commands when you are out on walks so he learns to go potty in different places. Some puppies learn that they are to relieve themselves only in the backyard, and their owners have a difficult time teaching them that it is okay to do it elsewhere. So teach your Dachsie that when you give him this command, he is to try, even if he can only squeeze out a drop!

When your Dachsie will relieve himself on command, you can take him traveling with you.

> ### Bet You Didn't Know _____
> Male dogs usually have no trouble relieving themselves in different places, because they are more prone to urinate to mark territory. With some male dogs, you'll have to curtail the marking, letting him know that you want him to relieve himself entirely in one spot, not on 20 different bushes all over the park!

Practicing Patience

New puppy owners seem to invite advice. Everyone who has ever owned a dog has a method of housetraining that works better or faster and is more reliable than anyone else's method. Ignore your well-meaning friends. All puppies need time to grow and develop bladder and bowel control. Just establish a schedule that seems to work for you and your Dachsie and stick to it. If you keep changing schedules or training techniques, you and your Dachsie will both be confused and frustrated.

If you follow the right schedule, your Dachsie will do fine. However, the lack of accidents doesn't mean you can back off on your supervision; instead, a lack of accidents means your schedule is good! If you back off too soon, your Dachsie will have some accidents and you'll have to start all over again.

A schedule that works for you and your Dachsie, along with careful supervision and lots of patience, will work. Puppies do grow up, and all your efforts will pay off when you find that you have a well-housetrained, reliable dog.

The Least You Need to Know

- 🐾 Teach your Dachsie to relieve himself outside, in a particular spot, and teach him a command to do so.
- 🐾 A crate is a wonderful training tool for housetraining.
- 🐾 Don't rub your Dachsie's nose in his accidents; instead, teach and supervise him better.
- 🐾 Establish a schedule, stick to it, and be patient.

Chapter 8

Introducing Your Dachshund to the World

In This Chapter

- 🏠 The importance of socialization
- 🏠 When and how to socialize
- 🏠 Understanding fear periods
- 🏠 Making socialization a lifelong activity

When properly socialized, a dog learns to deal with the world around him; the sights, sounds, and smells of the modern world as well as all of the different people. The world we live in is busy, chaotic, and full of challenges for people and dogs. The dog who is lucky enough to learn to deal with these challenges as a puppy will be better able to handle everything that comes his way.

However, the dog who isn't well socialized is more fearful of anything that is out of the ordinary, anything different. An unsocialized dog is less able to cope with the unexpected.

What Is Socialization?

Socialization, simply defined, is the process of introducing your Dachsie to the world around him. When a puppy or young dog meets people of all sizes, shapes, ages, and ethnic backgrounds, he will be less apt to shy away from people who are different. For example, many dogs who grow up in a home with only adults and are rarely exposed to children, often show shyness, fear, or aggression toward children. Having never really met children, these dogs seem to view children as creatures from another planet.

Dog Talk

Socialization is the process of introducing your dog to the world around him.

Although at times we may agree with that assessment, dogs showing poor behavior toward kids are potentially dangerous. It's important, then, that puppies meet people in all of their infinite varieties.

Dogs who aren't introduced to people as puppies and instead are isolated from people, especially during the critical 8- to 12-week age span, will never be able to form a good, strong attachment to people later. These dogs, even when born to dogs who were attached to people, will act more like wild animals than domesticated dogs.

Socialization encompasses more than just exposure to people, though. It also includes introducing your Dachsie to other dogs, especially dogs of other breeds, and other animals. Dachshunds recognize other Dachsies and, if not well socialized to dogs of other breeds, may not be friendly to them. Your Dachsie also needs to learn to tolerate the other animals in your family, including cats, rabbits, ferrets, and any other pets. If a neighbor or friend has a horse or a couple goats, introduce your Dachsie to those animals, too.

Socialization also includes the sights, sounds, and smells of the world. A sheet flapping on the clothesline might look like a really frightening thing initially, but if you show your Dachsie it's nothing serious, he will learn to investigate things that look different. A jack-hammer on the street, a motorcycle roaring by, and the clang of the garbage truck are all potentially scary sounds, but when they are introduced properly, your Dachsie can learn to deal with them.

The more your Dachsie sees, hears, and smells—without getting frightened—the better he will cope when faced with challenges as an adult.

Why Is Socialization So Important?

Your Dachsie's instincts tell him to trust his family members but not necessarily anyone else. Other people, dogs, or animals are either a threat, trespassers, or prey. Socialization teaches him that certain other people in certain situations are to be tolerated and perhaps even liked!

Because we ask so much of our dogs that is contrary to their ancient behaviors and working instincts, socialization is important; it gives the dog the skills to cope with our world.

Dachsie Wisdom
Socialization doesn't stop natural protective behavior; your Dachsie will still bark to warn you of trespassers. Socialization will, however, teach your dog which people should be considered a problem and which are friends.

At What Age Is Socialization Most Effective?

Basic social skills begin as early as the third week of life. At that age, your Dachsie discovers his brothers and sisters and learns to recognize them. They start interacting with each other—chewing on each other and wrestling. At this age your Dachsie also learns to recognize his mother as more than simply a source of food.

By the fourth and fifth week of life, your Dachsie is more aware of the world around him and interacts more and more with his mother and littermates. The mother starts correcting the puppies, and this social behavior teaches your Dachsie that life has rules that must be followed. He also learns that there are consequences to his actions—an important social lesson!

The breeder should be handling each puppy individually at this age to introduce them to human interactions. By massaging and cuddling the puppies, the breeder can teach the puppies that human touch is safe, comfortable, and pleasurable.

Watch Out!

The mother dog is vitally important to the puppies right now. Never buy or adopt a puppy who left his mother any earlier than five weeks old; behavior problems are very prevalent in these dogs as they grow up.

Dachsie Wisdom

You have to take time to do all the socialization necessary to prepare your puppy for life with you. You cannot be too busy right now; if you don't do this socialization now, you will never be able to make up for it later!

During the sixth and seventh weeks, the breeder must be very involved with the puppies, spending as much time as possible with them. The puppies can learn a lot about people now, and gentle handling is very important. Play time with people is also good, although the play must be gentle to help build trust in people. There should be no rough, tough, or scary play.

After you bring your puppy home, socialization continues to be very important. During the eighth through twelfth weeks of life, he needs to meet lots of different people and other pets and see and hear all the new (to him) things in this world. Socialization continues throughout puppyhood, but the time between 8 and 12 weeks of age is the most important.

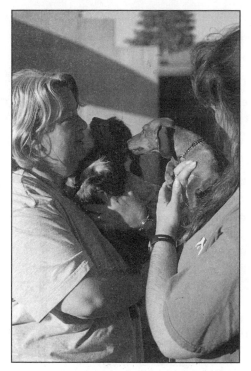

A part of socialization is meeting new people.

Fear Periods

During your Dachsie's eighth week of life, he will go through what is called a fear period. At this age, he has become very aware of the world around him, and sometimes that world is very scary. It's important that you try to prevent frightening things from happening at this age, but if they do, do not reinforce that fear. If you do, your Dachsie will remain afraid, and that fear will stay with him.

For example, if on the car ride home, he is frightened by a fire engine's siren, you should be matter-of-fact about it and try to distract him. If you cuddle him and murmur sweet things to him, he will take that as praise for being afraid. He will think that being afraid was the right response. Because you don't want him to be afraid of sirens and other loud shrill noises, distract him in a sensible, matter-of-fact way.

Puppies show they are in this fear period in many different ways. Some will become cautious about everything, approaching things (even familiar things) tentatively. Other puppies will be more selective—being bold about some things and cautious about others.

Bet You Didn't Know _____

We, as people, tend to try to comfort people or pets when they are afraid. We say, "Oh, it's okay, don't be afraid." Your Dachsie, however, will hear those soft words not as comfort but as a reinforcement that he was right to be afraid. Your comfort is telling him to be afraid!

You can do several different things to handle fear. First of all, talk to your puppy, but not in a soothing, "It's okay" tone of voice. Instead, your voice can be either calm and matter-of-fact, or you can use a higher pitched, fun tone of voice. You can distract your Dachsie by turning him away from whatever scared him and, when you turn him away, offer him a toy or a dog treat, "Here! What's this? Here's your ball!" Make him think about something else.

If the object of his fear is accessible, you might want to walk up to it, touch it, and show him it isn't as scary as he thought. Walk up to the motorcycle and pat it (as if you were petting it) and tell your Dachsie, "Come see!" If he walks close to it, praise him enthusiastically and tell him how brave he is! If he is really afraid, however, and plants his feet, don't force him up to the object of his fear. You can touch it, but let him sit back and look at it. When he's ready, then let him go up to it. If you force him, you may just make the fear that much worse.

Dachsie Wisdom _____

Plan your outings to make sure there aren't things that will frighten your puppy. Think about your destinations. Where can you go? What will your puppy see and hear there? Take some treats with you, too, and use them as a distraction when something happens that could be potentially frightening.

Your Dachsie will go through other fear periods as he grows up. Some puppies have a small fear period at about 4 months of age, and others go through one at about 14 months. You might think that a dog 14 months of age is grown up, but that's not true. A 14-month-old Dachshund is an adolescent—a teenager—and is still mentally immature. This is usually the last fear period most dogs go through; however, it should still be treated the same way you do with the puppies.

Watch Out! _____

Fear often makes no sense at all. Instead of trying to figure it out, just understand that the fear is real to your Dachshund, so work through it.

How to Socialize Your Dachshund

Much of your Dachsie's socialization can be as simple as allowing him to meet new people. Take him outside and introduce him to your neighbors. Let him meet the neighborhood kids, the retirees down the street, and the teenagers across the way. Let him meet people of all ages, sizes, shapes, and ethnic backgrounds. Introduce him to hats, floppy clothes, sunglasses, and other types of different clothing and accessories.

You can also plan outings so that he can go different places and meet other people:

🏠 Take him to the pet supply store and let him meet the sales clerks as well as other customers, then reward him by letting him pick out a new toy. In the pet supply store, he can also learn how to walk on slippery floors and see things he wouldn't see at home (like display shelves and stacks of aquariums). He can also learn to walk next to a shopping cart—something that is very different!

Even walking on different surfaces is a part of socialization.

🏠 Take him to the veterinarian's office even when he doesn't have an appointment. Just walk him in, have the receptionist give him a treat, then leave again. That makes the vet's office something special instead of something scary!

🏠 Pack up a picnic lunch, go to the local park and have a nice, quiet outing. You can sit on the blanket and read while your puppy chews on a toy. He can meet people who walk by, and he can watch and listen to the kids playing basketball.

- Go for a walk by the local elementary school while the kids are on recess. Let your Dachsie hear all the children laughing, screaming, and shouting. Let him watch them run and play. If you stop by after school, let one or two (*not* a whole crowd!) pet him very gently and give him a treat.

- Go for a walk by the local nursing or retirement home. If some of the residents are outside, introduce your puppy and ask if they would like to pet him.

- Ask your neighbor if your puppy can meet his or her pet rabbit. Hold your puppy carefully and encourage him to gently sniff the rabbit. Don't let him chase the bunny; remember you want to teach good manners! If you can, introduce him to other pets, including cats, ferrets, birds, and tortoises.

- If one of your neighbors has a healthy, well-vaccinated adult dog who is good with puppies, introduce the two. Let them play, if you can.

Watch Out!
Be aware of your Dachsie's natural hunting instincts as you introduce him to other animals. Do *not* allow him to chase or attack your neighbor's pet rabbit!

Watch Out!
Don't introduce your Dachsie to every dog in town; be selective. Socialize only with healthy, well-vaccinated, well-behaved dogs who are safe with puppies and small dogs. Don't be afraid to ask questions in order to protect your Dachsie.

Dachshunds instinctively recognize each other, but they must be introduced to dogs of other breeds.

Training Classes

You might want to consider enrolling your Dachshund puppy in a kindergarten puppy training class. Not only will this help you train your puppy, but it's wonderful socialization to other puppies and other people.

Dachsie Wisdom

Sometimes socialization takes planning, but it is something that is very important to your puppy's future, so make the time for it now, when it's most effective!

If your Dachsie is too old for a puppy class, he can still meet other dogs and people at a basic obedience training class.

What Should Your Puppy See, Smell, and Hear?

Introduce your puppy to as much as you can—not all at once, of course, but throughout puppyhood. Let him become familiar, comfortable, and confident about the world around him.

Protecting him from harm (without reinforcing fear), let him see, hear, or smell ...

- 🏠 Household appliances, including the vacuum cleaner, dishwasher, garbage disposer, and trash compactor.

- 🏠 A broom and a mop being used.

- 🏠 Household tools in use, including a hammer, saw, sander, or other commonly used tools.

- 🏠 A plastic garbage bag being shaken open and a crumpled paper bag.

- 🏠 A metal cookie sheet being dropped to the floor.

- 🏠 The garbage truck out front and a motorcycle zooming down the street.

- 🏠 Yard tools, including a lawn mower, a weed whacker, and leaf blower.

- 🏠 Children's toys, including some that make noise, as well as balls and flying discs.

- 🏠 Balloons.

Dachsie Wisdom

Your Dachsie's adult personality is shaped by several things: his breed and genetic heritage, his mother's care, the socialization and training he receives, and you.

What else is a part of your life—that will be part of your puppy's life—that he needs to be comfortable with?

What *Not* to Do

Don't try to introduce your Dachshund to everything all at once. Overwhelming him is just as bad as not socializing him. Socialization should be a gradual process taking place over the first few months of his life.

In his first week at home (and it doesn't matter whether he is a puppy or an adult Dachsie), introduce him to things around the house. That way, you can make sure he isn't frightened or, if he is, that you don't reinforce those fears. Keep things upbeat, happy, and matter-of-fact.

During his second week at home, take him outside a little more, introduce him to a few things around the neighborhood, and let him meet some new people. There are some things you must control, however, to protect your Dachsie:

- 🏠 Don't let kids run, scream, and yell while playing with your Dachsie. Again, this is overstimulating or scary.

- 🏠 Don't let people grab your Dachsie away from you and hug him tightly.

- 🏠 Don't let kids throw themselves on your Dachsie or grab at him.

- 🏠 Don't allow people to blow in his face or stare at him.

- 🏠 Don't let people treat him roughly.

Watch Out!

You *must always* control interactions between your Dachsie and other people. Never let people get rough with your Dachsie for any reason, even in play. If you think something is wrong, stop it. If you have to, pick up your Dachsie and walk away.

Remember, the whole idea is to make these outings fun and to build social skills, not to scare your Dachsie.

Each week, you can do more and introduce him to different things. Just take it slow and gradual and, if your Dachsie seems overwhelmed, stop and relax for a little while.

When Your Veterinarian Says "Keep Him at Home!"

If your Dachshund is young, your veterinarian will probably tell you to keep him home until he has finished all his vaccinations. Until then, he may be at risk of picking up a contagious disease from unvaccinated, unhealthy dogs. However, I have just finished telling you to take your Dachsie out into the world, introduce him to people and other animals, and worse yet, enroll him in a kindergarten puppy class! Obviously, there is a conflict here!

Your veterinarian is concerned about your puppy's health. As a dog trainer, I am concerned about the serious consequences of a lack of socialization. Every year, thousands of dogs are given up by their owners because of behavior problems. Now not all of those are the result of a lack of socialization, but a great many of them are. You can socialize your dog and keep him safe, too. What we can do is try and work a compromise with your veterinarian, keeping your Dachsie as safe as possible yet getting him the socialization he needs.

First of all, don't take him anywhere there are other dogs, especially potentially unvaccinated dogs, until your Dachsie puppy has had at least two full sets of shots. These vaccines should include distemper, hepatitis, leptospirosis, parvovirus, and parainfluenza. Most puppies have, at that point, good immunities. Most kindergarten puppy classes will not allow puppies to attend until they have had these two sets of shots.

When you take your Dachsie out in public, ask questions of dog owners *before* you let the dogs sniff each other, "When were your dog's last shots?" If they get upset, too bad! It's your puppy's health, and you have every right to protect him.

Most of the dangers to your puppy's health come from unvaccinated dogs and their wastes. Keep him away from unknown dogs, and don't let your puppy sniff other dogs' feces and urine. Keep him away, and pull him away if he tries to sniff.

You can keep your Dachsie puppy safe by being aware and careful, yet still get him the socialization he needs for good mental health.

Socialization Is an Ongoing Process

Although the most important socialization period is during early puppyhood, socialization is an ongoing process until your Dachsie's second birthday. Most Dachshunds aren't mentally grown up until they are at least two years old, and socialization is a big part of that mental maturity.

I am always exposing my dogs—even my adult dogs—to different things. On any given weekend, we may play on the playground, go to a different park, meet a parade horse, or watch a marching band. My dogs have swum in the ocean, sniffed noses with a Budweiser Clydesdale, visited with Alzheimer's patients, and ridden on a San Francisco cable car. And they take it all in stride because we continue to do different things.

My grandmother always said that parents should raise their children to take the path they want them to take. Basically, it's the same with Dachshund puppies. Raise your puppy to take that path with you; if you like to do things and go places, introduce your Dachsie to those things now and, when he's grown up, he'll be right there by your side.

The Least You Need to Know

- 🏠 Socialization is the process of introducing your Dachshund to the world around him, including people of all sizes, shapes, ages, and ethnic backgrounds.

- 🏠 Your Dachsie also needs to see, hear, and smell different things.

- 🏠 Socialization is an ongoing process, but is especially important between 8 and 12 weeks of age.

- 🏠 During socialization, it's important to protect your puppy without reinforcing his fears.

Part 3

Keeping Your Dachshund Healthy

A healthy Dachshund is a happy Dachshund! Plus, you'll be happier when your dog is healthy. There is nothing quite as sad as a dog who doesn't feel well; those sad eyes just tear you apart. So let's begin by talking about what keeps your dog healthy and how to work with your veterinarian—who should be your partner in your dog's health care.

Most people assume only dogs with coats like a Poodle need grooming, but all dogs—even short-haired ones—need to be groomed. Brushing, combing, cleaning ears, trimming toenails, and brushing teeth are all a part of the regular grooming process that will help keep your Dachsie clean and healthy.

This part will answer your questions about your dog's health and health care, including nutrition, vaccinations and diseases, parasites, and emergency first aid. We'll also discuss that problem all Dachshund owners must be aware of—the fragility of that long back—and how to keep it healthy.

Fresh water and high-quality food will help keep your Dachsie healthy.

Chapter 9

Maintaining Your Dachshund's Health

In This Chapter

🏠 The importance of exercise and the fun of playtime

🏠 Spaying and neutering

🏠 Working with your veterinarian

🏠 Taking care of your Dachsie

Maintaining your Dachsie's good health is an ongoing project. Exercise is just as important for your Dachsie as it is for you, especially to keep that long back fit and healthy. Play may seem frivolous, but it's a vital part of your relationship and your Dachsie's good mental and physical health. Spaying and neutering is also important for several reasons, all of which we will discuss.

Your veterinarian is your partner in your Dachsie's good health. This begins with your Dachsie's first visit to the vet's office and continues throughout your dog's life. You'll find some ideas as to how to work with your vet to maintain your Dachsie's good health.

Exercise and Playtime

A healthy young Dachshund will need several exercise sessions every day. He will need time to use up energy, burn calories, and strengthen his bones and muscles. This exercise will also help him learn to control his body and become more coordinated.

Exercise for a young puppy must be tailored carefully to the puppy's age, physical abilities, and breed. A 10-week-old miniature Dachsie puppy is very tiny and fragile but is, by way of his build, much more coordinated than the much larger but more rapidly growing standard Dachshund puppy. The mini Dachsie puppy will be able to move faster, balance himself better, and twist and turn better than the larger puppy. The standard, because of his larger size, will not be nearly as coordinated, at least during puppyhood.

Exercise is important for your Dachsie's good health.

When exercising your Dachsie, make sure he can do the exercise without getting sore or overly tired. A nap after exercise is normal, but an exhausted extended sleep is not. For example, if you and the puppy go for a neighborhood walk and the puppy quits mid-walk and refuses to get back up, you've gone too far.

Exercise Ideas

Exercise ideas for young puppies 8 to 12 weeks of age:

- Walk around the neighborhood.
- Walk around the local park, harbor, shopping center, or school.
- Take a short, easy hike in the local woods or meadow.
- Throw the tennis ball (short throws).

Exercise ideas for puppies 12 to 18 weeks of age:

- Walk for a slightly longer period.
- Jog for a very short time on a soft surface such as grass.
- Climb on playground equipment—carefully assisted and supervised, of course!
- Take slightly longer hikes in the woods or other wild lands.

Exercise ideas for older puppies:

- Very gradually increase the distance and speed of walks.
- Very gradually increase the distance and speed of jogs.

Watch Out!

Limit your Dachsie's jumping (especially jumping down from things) and twisting motions to protect his back. His bones are still growing and forming at this age.

Playtime Is for Fun!

Playtime can be a part of exercise, especially if you play retrieving games with your Dachsie, but playtime can be separate from exercise. Playtime is fun time, and the fun that you and your Dachsie have together helps create the bond between the two of you. Shared experiences—including play—cement that bond, that relationship.

Some play ideas for young puppies:

🏠 Lie on the floor and roll the puppy over, rub his tummy, and roll him back and forth. Let him squirm and flail his legs. Laugh with him, talk baby talk to him, and call him silly names.

Watch Out!

Don't wrestle with your Dachsie. Wrestling teaches him to fight you and to use his strength against you. This is always a bad idea.

🏠 Play short, quick retrieving games with different toys.

🏠 Play easy, short hide-and-seek games.

Some play ideas for slightly older puppies:

🏠 Make the retrieving games slightly longer.

🏠 Make the hide-and-seek games slightly more difficult but still easily accomplishable.

🏠 Teach the puppy some fun tricks, like shake, roll over, or speak.

🏠 Teach the puppy the names of his toys, such as ball, bone, or squeaker.

Some play ideas for adult Dachshunds:

🏠 Lots of retrieving games with different toys.

🏠 More difficult hide-and-seek games.

Bet You Didn't Know

Playing tug-of-war with your Dachsie teaches him to use his jaws and his strength against you. Because he is already a hunter by instinct, this can be a poor choice of games. Instead, play games that require his co-operation with you instead of his fighting against you.

🏠 Play dog activities and sports, such as agility and flyball.

🏠 Encourage your Dachsie to chase you as you zigzag around the yard. Do *not* chase him, however, as it teaches him to run from you!

Playtime is fun for you and your Dachsie and is also good for your relationship.

Playtime should be fun and filled with petting, hugs, and laughter. Play can be good exercise, too, and can be wonderful mental stimulation, but the most important part of play is the fun that you can your Dachsie have together.

Let's Talk About Spaying and Neutering

Most Dachshunds should be spayed (females) or neutered (males). The only ones who should be bred are those who are the best in physical conformation, temperament, genetic health, and working characteristics. By only breeding the best of the breed, you're helping make sure that future puppies are healthier, with fewer genetic defects, and with good sound temperaments.

Breeding is a huge undertaking. To do it right, the potential breeding dogs must be investigated as to their physical, mental, and emotional health, as well as their genetic health. What about their working instincts? That must be there, too, or the breed will not remain the same. Plus, there can be complications during the breeding process, during the pregnancy, or during and after the puppies' births. Are you ready to bottle-raise a litter, for example? Do you know what care will be needed during the first few days of life? To be a responsible breeder, there's a lot you need to know and do.

Unfortunately, many people breed their dogs, or allow their dogs to breed, without knowing what needs to be done as a responsible breeder. The end result has been hundreds of thousands of dogs born only to be destroyed. Some are "put to sleep" because there weren't enough homes available for all of them, while others were euthanized because of health or temperament problems.

Each and every dog who is given up as unwanted, who becomes a stray, or who is involved in a dog bite situation ends up costing taxpayers money. Because of this, many cities and counties across the United States are trying to regulate dog breeding. Many have instituted fines or costly licenses to discourage dog breeding.

These measures may hamper or discourage the reputable, responsible breeder but, unfortunately, won't do anything to control indiscriminate, accidental breedings. However, a spayed or neutered dog cannot reproduce, even accidentally!

Bet You Didn't Know

Spaying and neutering your pet does cost money, although it is usually very reasonable and discounted programs are available all over the country. However, you'll get that cost back by paying reduced dog license fees once your pet is spayed or neutered.

Traditionally, dogs have been spayed or neutered at about six months of age. However, many humane societies—in an effort to discourage breeding—have been spaying and neutering very young puppies, some as young as eight weeks of age. This has been very successful and has shown to have no ill effects on the puppy's health.

What Happens?

Spaying a female dog consists of a surgical ovariohysterectomy. The ovaries and uterus are removed through an incision in the abdomen.

Your veterinarian will tell you to keep her quiet for a few days, but most dogs don't show any signs of discomfort and recuperate very quickly. Her stitches will come out in about 10 days.

A male dog is neutered (castrated). This consists of removing the testicles through an incision just in front of the scrotum. Again, your vet will tell you to keep the puppy quiet for a few days, and that could be difficult because the puppy won't appear to be uncomfortable at all.

 Dachsie Wisdom

A female who has been spayed will no longer go through her "season," that two- to three-times-per-year hassle. She will no longer spot on your floors and carpets, and male dogs will no longer "come calling"!

 Dachsie Wisdom

Have you heard that a spayed or neutered dog will get fat? Well that's a myth. Too much food and not enough exercise cause dogs to get fat!

Other Health Benefits

There are other health benefits of spaying and neutering besides stopping reproduction:

For females:

🏠 Decreases incidences of breast or mammary gland cancers.

🏠 Protects her against cancers of the reproductive system.

🏠 Decreases the incidences of female aggression.

For males:

🏠 Decreases male sexual behaviors, including leg-lifting, marking, roaming, and fighting.

🏠 Decreases the urge to escape the yard.

🏠 Protects him from testicular cancers.

Working with Your Veterinarian

Your veterinarian is vitally important to your Dachshund's continued good health. In Chapter 5, we discussed how to find a veterinarian and the importance of making contact with her prior to bringing home your Dachsie. Hopefully you did so and now feel comfortable with this vet, her staff, and her policies.

Your Dachshund should go in to see the veterinarian within the first 24 hours after you bring him home. This accomplishes several things. First, this visit can assure you of your new dog's state of health and can pinpoint any potential health problems. If your Dachshund has come with a health guarantee, this is important so that contract is valid.

There is the possibility your vet could find congenital health problems you are unaware of. If the Dachsie has untreatable or potentially expensive health problems or is genetically unhealthy, you have the right (if you so desire) to return the puppy to the breeder. If the puppy has a problem and you decide to keep him anyway, the breeder should be willing to give you a full or partial refund.

> **Watch Out!**
> Make sure you read the breeder's sales contract carefully. Many require that a puppy with health problems be returned to the breeder for a refund, reimbursement, or replacement.

If you adopted your Dachsie from a shelter or a rescue group, there will be no health guarantee. However, if there are drastic health problems, you may decide to return the dog before you are too emotionally attached to him.

If you decide to keep this Dachsie, even with health problems, knowing about them early can help you plan for them. And most important perhaps, budget for them!

The First Exam

When you bring your Dachsie in for his first exam, bring a stool (feces) sample with you. This can be processed during your visit so that if your Dachsie has some internal parasites, medication can be prescribed while you are there. This way, you won't need to make a second trip.

The first visit will be quite thorough. Not only do you need to know as much about this dog as possible, but your vet does, too. Give her as much information as you can—date of birth, any information the breeder may have given you about the puppy's health, and any vaccinations the breeder, shelter, or rescue group may have given.

Bet You Didn't Know
Some dog owners seem to begrudge the money spent at the veterinarian's office, saying that the vet is only after their money. Certainly, the vet does need to earn a living, just as you and I do; however, your vet is also dedicated to maintaining your Dachsie's good health. Let her help you do it!

This is also the time to ask questions. If you have any concerns about the puppy's health, diet, energy, activity levels, or anything else, ask them now.

Vaccinations

Your veterinarian will also set up a vaccination schedule for your Dachsie depending on what vaccinations might or might not have already been given. Vaccinations work by giving the body a weakened dose of the disease so the dog can develop the right antibodies (disease-fighting cells) without the threat of getting sick. Most *vaccines* stimulate the body into producing antibodies for a period of time. Booster shots are then given to continue the protection.

Dog Talk
Vaccines are either modified-live or killed. Modified-live vaccines are considered more effective but carry a risk of transmitting the disease.

Watch Out!
Parvovirus is the most deadly, dangerous, and fatal disease known to dogs.

Vaccinations are available for distemper, hepatitis, leptospirosis, coronavirus, parvovirus, adenovirus, parainfluenza, bordatella, Lyme disease, and rabies. These diseases are discussed in detail in Chapter 12.

Which Vaccines?

Your veterinarian will make some recommendations for vaccinations, depending on where you live and which diseases are seen in your

Dachsie Wisdom
The Dachsie is your dog, so ask as many questions as you want. Your vet should not be threatened by questions.

region. For example, if coronavirus isn't seen in your area, your vet may not feel it's worth vaccinating your dog for it. However, if you will be traveling to an area where the disease is seen, you should tell your vet that.

Potential Problems with Vaccines

Even though modern vaccines have saved thousands of dogs' lives, that doesn't mean there is no risk associated with them. Unfortunately, there is.

The most common side effect of vaccinations is a small, hard bump at the injection site that shows up a few days afterward. This is called a sterile abscess and will go away on its own.

Some dogs, though, suffer an allergic reaction to some vaccines. It may be as mild as some shivering and a fever, or it may be as severe as anaphylactic shock—which can be life-threatening. You should always remain in the vet's office for at least 30 minutes after your Dachsie receives an injection, as most reactions—especially severe ones—will show up within 30 minutes. Immediate treatment is vital to save your Dachsie should he have a severe reaction.

Too Much of a Good Thing?

Many veterinarians and dog owners are concerned that too many vaccinations may be damaging dogs' immune systems. Years ago, dogs were vaccinated only for distemper and rabies. Today, your Dachsie may receive six or eight vaccines. This can have a debilitating effect on the immune system.

Therefore, talk to your vet and ask his opinion. He may recommend a different vaccination schedule. Some vets are giving boosters every 18 months rather than every 12, as is often recommended.

Just because there may be problems associated with vaccines doesn't mean you shouldn't have your dog vaccinated, however. The risks of your Dachshund dying from diseases are much higher than any risk associated with vaccinations.

Only Vaccinate a Healthy Dog

To keep risks low, don't vaccinate a dog or puppy who isn't feeling well. If you take your Dachsie to the vet's office for diarrhea or another problem, don't try to save money (an office fee) by having the dog vaccinated at the same time. Not only will the vaccine stress the dog's already threatened immune system, but the vaccine may not work as well since the dog is sick already.

Recognizing Potential Problems

Many healthy Dachsie puppies grow up to be healthy adults that see the veterinarian once per year for an annual check-up; for healthy dogs, this schedule is absolutely fine. However, you may need to bring your Dachsie in if he develops a problem of some kind. Recognizing those problems is important, because catching something early may save you, your Dachsie, and your veterinarian considerable grief.

Call your veterinarian if you notice any of these potential problems:

🏠 Vomiting that doesn't stop after a couple hours.

🏠 Diarrhea that continues more than one day, or that contains a lot of mucus or any blood.

🏠 A temperature lower than 100 degrees or above 102.5 degrees.

🏠 Fainting, collapse, or a seizure.

🏠 Severe coughing, trouble breathing, or a suspected obstruction.

🏠 The puppy refuses to eat and misses more than two meals.

🏠 A leg that is obviously hurt, with no weight on it, and is still held up after you massage it gently.

🏠 A distended abdomen and obvious tenderness.

🏠 Any eye injury.

🏠 Potential allergic reactions, including swelling, hives, or rashes, especially around the face.

🏠 Potential poisonings, especially antifreeze, rodent poisons, snail poisons, insecticides, or herbicides.

🏠 Cuts or wounds that are bleeding and gape open or that don't stop bleeding with direct pressure.

🏠 Suspected snake bites or bites of any kind.

Some things might not be quite as noticeable but could still signal trouble. Call your vet if you see any of these signs:

Watch Out!

Never ignore one of these trouble signs, hoping they will go away. They might, of course, but they might not, and that wasted time could make the problem that much worse for your Dachsie.

🏠 The puppy is hiding and doesn't want to come out.

🏠 Panting other than after exercise or playtime.

🏠 Heavy breathing for no apparent reason.

🏠 No energy.

🏠 Restlessness for no apparent reason.

🏠 Sudden loss of appetite.

What Your Vet Will Want to Know

When you call your veterinarian, the receptionist will ask you several questions. It's her job to get as much information as possible and pass it on the vet. Don't give her a hard time, argue with her, or insist on talking to the vet. Answer her questions with as much detail as you can. She will then talk to the vet and have some answers or advice for you, or the vet will come back on the line to talk to you.

Some questions you will be expected to answer include the following:

🏠 What is the specific problem?

🏠 What made you notice it?

🏠 What are the symptoms?

🏠 What's the puppy's rectal temperature?

🏠 Has the puppy eaten? When? What? How much?

🏠 Is there any vomiting? Diarrhea? What does it look like?

🏠 Did you catch the puppy digging through the trash? Were you camping and the puppy drank from a stream?

🏠 How long has this problem been going on?

Give your veterinarian too much information rather than too little. Let him wade through the information and decide what's relevant and what isn't—that's where his expertise comes into play. Your job is to supply him with enough information so he can help you and your Dachsie.

Giving Your Dachsie Medication

Giving your Dachsie medication isn't always easy, but there are some tricks to make it easier. If at all possible, keep this as stress-free as you can. If your Dachsie learns to hate medication and treatments now, as a puppy, he will retain that hatred throughout his life, and that could be very difficult.

Giving pills, tablets, and capsules is actually one of the easier medications to administer. If the medication may be given with food, simply hide the medication in a bit of food and let your Dachsie eat it. Some good foods for hiding pills include bits of hot dogs, peanut butter, sliced cheese, and commercial dog treats.

Liquid medication can be more difficult to give and much messier. Ask your vet for plastic droppers or a few large plastic syringes without needles. Measure the medication into the syringe, then place the end of the syringe in the side of the puppy's mouth between the back teeth. Squirt the medication in slowly, giving the puppy time to swallow.

Watch Out!
When giving liquid medication, don't try to force the puppy's mouth open. The medication will end up all over you and the puppy!

Watch Out!
Follow directions for all medications. If it is to be used or given 3 times a day for 10 days, give it 3 times a day for 10 days. Anything more or less could endanger your Dachsie's health.

Eye medication takes a sure, swift, gentle touch. If you fool around, your Dachsie will get nervous. Try this trick: Take a spoonful of peanut butter and scrape it off on the roof of the Dachsie's mouth behind the front teeth. As your Dachsie licks this and tries to swallow it, gently hold her head and apply the medication.

The peanut butter trick works well for ear medications, too. While the puppy is thinking about the peanut butter, gently wipe out his ear with a cotton ball and apply the medication according to the vet's instructions.

If your Dachsie has a cut or incision that must be washed, treated, or medicated, you can use the peanut butter trick here, too. Just be very gentle, sure, and quick (not tentative) as you wash and medicate it.

Taking Reasonable Care

Hopefully you puppy-proofed your house and yard prior to bringing home your Dachsie. If you did, there shouldn't be too many dangers there. However, Dachshunds can be inventive, tenacious, and down right surprising sometimes, especially for first-time Dachsie owners. Dachsies can get up on counters, workbenches in the garage, and other shelves where they really shouldn't be able to climb—but they do! They also learn to open cupboard doors, chew their way into boxes, and pull stuff down off shelves. Dachsies can and do get into trouble, and that trouble can endanger their lives!

You can prevent many accidents simply by taking precautions and reasonable care.

However, you can prevent as much as possible from happening if you look at the world through your Dachsie's eyes. Make sure anything poisonous or dangerous is put away—really away—where your Dachsie *cannot* reach it. Put latches on cupboard doors. Make sure the trash is unreachable. Do car repairs where the puppy can't get into the oil, grease, gasoline, or antifreeze—all of these are deadly, especially antifreeze, of which a lick or two is enough to kill your Dachsie. By being proactive and eliminating as many dangers as realistically possible, you can keep your Dachsie safe.

Common sense also plays a big part in keeping your Dachsie safe. If you take your Dachsie to the woods, check him thoroughly for ticks when you come home. If he's playing in long grass, look for burrs and foxtails (grass seeds that stick in the coat). If there is broken glass on the ground, take him somewhere else to play. Don't let him play off leash if there is a street nearby or if he doesn't come when you call him. Use your common sense to keep your Dachsie safe.

The Least You Need to Know

- Appropriate exercise and playtimes will use up energy, help your Dachsie's strength and coordination, and give you an additional way to strengthen the bond between you and your Dachsie.

- Spaying and neutering your Dachsie will help avoid unwanted and unneeded puppies, decrease the incidences of unwanted sexual behaviors, and also help with your Dachsie's long term health.

- Your veterinarian can help you keep your Dachsie healthy.

- Reasonable care and common sense can prevent accidents and dangers that threaten your Dachsie.

Chapter 10

Routine Care from Nose to Tail

In This Chapter

- 🏠 Regular grooming tips
- 🏠 Bathing and trimming toenails
- 🏠 Cleaning ears and brushing teeth
- 🏠 The daily massage

A healthy Dachshund is a bright, alert dog who looks the picture of health. Certainly, good genetics is a part of good health, as are regular veterinary exams and vaccinations. But good health also requires some routine care.

Some health chores should become a part of your weekly and daily routines so you don't procrastinate or forget to do them. For example, if toenails are trimmed each weekend, they will not overgrow, causing your Dachsie foot pain. In addition, by cutting his nails regularly, you'll help your dog get used to the chore, and he will not fight you when you do it.

As you begin making these health-care chores a part of your routine, teach your Dachsie to accept them willingly. This way, they will not turn into problems. After all, your Dachsie cannot care for himself—that's your job!

All Dachsies Need Grooming

Many dog owners feel that grooming only applies to Poodles and Spaniels who go to the grooming salon for haircuts. However, dog experts refer to grooming as the body care that encompasses bathing, brushing, combing, dematting, haircuts, and trimming. All dogs, regardless of breed and coat type, require some grooming. Some breeds, of course, like Poodles and Spaniels, do require more.

Many people recognize that the wirehaired and longhaired Dachsies need grooming, but the smooth dogs need to be groomed, too. Smooth Dachsies can shed just as much as their longer-haired cousins. And contrary to popular belief, short hair isn't always easier to deal with. Whereas longer hair tends to ball up, forming those infamous dog hair dust bunnies, short hair is prickly and sticks to things, including sofa cushions, pillows, clothes, and even human skin!

Smooth-Coat Grooming

Smooth-coated Dachsies should be brushed daily. A soft-bristle brush can be used to get most of the dead hair out of the coat. Make sure you brush all over the dog—from the head to the tip of the tail. Not only does brushing get rid of the dead hair, it also stimulates the skin, keeping the hair coat healthy. Many people like to finish the job with a damp wash cloth to get off the last of the shedding hair. The damp cloth also gives the coat a nice shine.

Longhaired Grooming

The longhaired coat needs regular grooming to keep it looking nice. As with most dogs who have a silky coat, this silky coat can tangle and matt. These matts are most apt to form where the dog's body parts move against one another, such as under the front legs and between the back legs. They also form behind the ears and under the collar on the neck.

Begin grooming the longhaired Dachsie by going over him with a bristle or pin brush. Work out as many of the small tangles as you can with the brush. When you have found a larger tangle the brush can't work out, use a comb or matt splitter to work at it. If the tangle is stubborn and in a spot where trimming the coat won't show, you can cut the matt out. Just place your fingers between the matt and the dog's skin so you don't cut the dog and then very carefully, using tiny snips, trim the matt out.

Once the matts are out, use a comb to go through the coat, finishing the overall look. Make sure the ears and tail are combed, too. Occasionally, you may want to trim some overgrown hairs, such as those between the pads of the feet. Just do so carefully, making sure not to cut any skin.

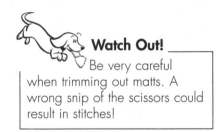

Watch Out!
Be very careful when trimming out matts. A wrong snip of the scissors could result in stitches!

Wirehaired Grooming

The coarse wirehaired coat needs a totally different type of grooming than the smooth or longhaired coat. This coarse, terrier coat can be either hand-stripped or groomed with clippers. The correct grooming for a conformation show dog is hand-stripping, but this is a difficult skill to learn, and many professional groomers don't do it. Therefore, many pet owners simply have their wirehaired Dachsie's coat cut close with clippers.

When a coat is hand-stripped, the dead hair coat (which is already loose) is pulled out. Some people use their fingers, catching the hairs between the thumb and the first two fingers. Some people use a stripping knife. The entire dog is stripped, with all the dead hairs pulled out of the coat. Stripping can take several hours, so it's usually a good idea to do it in several sessions. Otherwise, your Dachsie will get wiggly, impatient, and will resent the process. Dogs who are hand-stripped are usually done twice a year—spring and fall.

When a wirehaired dog is groomed with clippers, the groomer may shave him with a ⅜- or ¼-inch blade, depending on your preference. The dog then ends up the same length all over, although many groomers leave more length on the muzzle and tail.

Dachsie Wisdom

Many Dachsie owners say that cutting the hair with clippers changes the coat, making it softer, less wiry, and the color may change. Not everyone agrees that these changes happen, though, so it might depend on the individual dog.

Dog Talk

A **groomer** is a person whose career is to care for the skin and coat of dogs, cats, and other pets. A groomer knows how to brush out coats, dematt them (when possible), and what type of haircut each breed should have (when needed).

How you decide to groom your dog depends on your personal preference. Hand-stripping is very time-consuming. However, if you like the wirehaired coat and texture, you might want to learn how to hand-strip it. If you want a coat that is easier to care for, you may want to have a professional *groomer* shave your dog. It's up to you.

If you decide to use a groomer's services, you will want to introduce your Dachsie to the groomer and his or her place of business. Bring a few treats with you when you go to the shop, and encourage the receptionist, the groomer, and other staff members to give him treats, scratch his ears, pet him, and make a fuss over him. You want him to like going to the groomer's!

One the second or third trip there, let the groomer put him up on the grooming table and comb or brush him. The groomer can offer him a treat at the same time. Again, you want this to be a very positive experience, because your Dachsie will be going there on a regular basis.

When you leave him for his first haircut, try to arrange with the groomer to leave him for just a couple hours and not much longer. Although most adult dogs spend the day at the groomer's salon, that's too much for a puppy, especially for the first haircut.

Grooming Tools

Grooming tools come in a variety of sizes, shapes, and uses. Some are right for certain hair coats and not for others. It's important that you know what tools are appropriate for your Dachsie's coat.

- 🐾 **Combs.** Combs are used to go through the coat to smooth it or to help remove small tangles. Most are metal with closely spaced teeth on one side and wider spaced teeth on the other. Combs don't have much value on smooth Dachsies but are useful for longhaired and wirehaired Dachsies.

- 🐾 **Flea combs.** These have very fine, closely spaced teeth that drag fleas out of the coat. These work well on all three coat types.

- 🐾 **Pin brush.** A pin brush has spaced teeth mounted on a rubber pad. The teeth are either flat-topped or topped with a tiny round head. Pin brushes are fine for wirehaired and longhaired Dachsies—they will help pull dead hair out of the coat and ease out tangles.

- 🐾 **Slicker brush.** This brush has teeth that are of relatively fine wire and are bent at an angle about halfway along their length. These brushes are good for the top coat but don't reach deep into a long coat. The slicker is too rough and sharp for a smooth Dachsie.

- **Bristle brush.** This has pig hair, horse hair, or synthetic bristles. Many bristles are crowded together to make a dense surface brush. This is particularly good for a smooth Dachsie.

- **Dematter.** This brush has three, four, or five blades, usually about an inch and a half long, that are sharp on one side. It is used on the thick hair around the dog's neck and the back of the legs and to split any tangles or matts. It will also drag out any dead or shedding coat.

If you have any questions about what tools might work best or if you aren't quite sure how to use them, make an appointment with your groomer. Expect to pay her for her time, but ask her to show you the correct way to use the tools on your Dachsie. Because your correct use of them will make her job easy, she should be more than happy to help you.

Brushing Your Dachsie

The mechanics of brushing aren't very difficult. Sit on the floor and invite your Dachsie to lie down on your lap or between your legs. Give him some peanut butter (if he needs it) to distract him and start brushing on his head. Using a comb, soft-bristle brush, or pin brush, start gently brushing the hair in the direction it grows in. Go with the hair, not against it.

If your Dachsie has short hair, use your soft-bristle brush and, after brushing the head very gently, start working down around the ears, to the neck, shoulders, and down the back. Gently brush portions of the body, then let your Dachsie up to praise him. When the entire body has been brushed and the coat is clean, he's done.

For wirehaired and longhaired Dachsies, a little more effort is involved to work through the hair, but the process is similar. Begin brushing and combing at the head and work down the body.

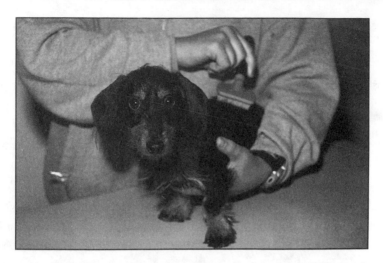

All Dachsies need grooming, no matter what the coat type.

Bathing Your Dachsie

Dachsies are always getting into stuff, whether it's mud or dirt from a gopher hole or dust balls under the sofa. Bathing your Dachsie regularly—weekly, if necessary—will keep him clean and smelling fresh.

There are many dog shampoos available commercially. Read the labels, and make sure the shampoo is appropriate for your dog's age and condition. If you have a puppy, make sure the shampoo is recommended for puppies. Don't get a medicated shampoo unless your veterinarian recommends it. Don't use an insecticide shampoo, either, unless your Dachsie actually has fleas. Whatever kind of shampoo you need, make sure it's good quality.

Mini Dachsies can be bathed in the sink, but standards will need to be bathed in the bathtub. A handheld shower nozzle works well to get the dog completely wet and then rinsed thoroughly.

Brush or comb your Dachsie thoroughly before you bathe him. Make sure all tangles are out of his coat, because water turns tangles into cement, and you'll have to cut them out after the bath. Before

Dachsie Wisdom

Consider putting a nonslip rubber sheet in the tub to keep your Dachsie from slipping. If your Dachsie struggles, giving him treats throughout the bath might help calm him down.

you put your Dachsie in the tub, grab a few towels, the shampoo, and some cotton balls. Put a cotton ball into each of his ears to help keep the ears dry. Set the water to a nice comfortable temperature, and lift the dog in. If he struggles, try calm him with your voice, but don't let him struggle or fight you.

Use the handheld nozzle to thoroughly wet him, then turn the water off. Work the shampoo into his coat, then rinse him off. On his head, run the water away from his eyes and ears. Make sure all the soap is rinsed out.

When he's thoroughly rinsed, towel him off very well and then, if he'll let you, keep him wrapped up in the towel for a few minutes while you cuddle him. Let him warm up a little. If the weather or your house is chilly, use the blow dryer on a low setting for a few minutes to dry him and warm him up.

Special Grooming Problems

If your Dachsie gets into chewing gum or oil or meets a skunk, a normal bath isn't going to solve the problem. Here are some special grooming suggestions:

- **Burrs, foxtails, and other seeds.** These often can be combed out. If they're in a tangle, use just a little vegetable oil or hair conditioner to make the burr slippery. You will then have to wash the oil or conditioner out; use Joy dish soap or a good shampoo. If the seed is really worked into the coat, trim it out.

- **Fleas.** A flea comb will catch some of the little pests, especially around the puppy's eyes and ears. Insecticides (for use on puppies) also work, but many owners are afraid of using too much, and it's a legitimate concern. Talk to your veterinarian about his recommendations for flea control. There are many alternatives available.

🏠 **Gum or other sticky stuff.** Use some ice to freeze it and break it out or some vegetable oil to ooze it out. Gum usually needs to be trimmed out.

🏠 **Motor oil.** Joy dish soap will usually cut the oil. Just make sure you rinse it out well.

Watch Out!
Flea and tick products—both those used on the dog and those for use in the house and yard—can be potentially dangerous to your dog. Read labels carefully and use with caution.

🏠 **Paint.** Don't use paint solvents—they're toxic! Try to wash the paint out and, if that doesn't work, trim away the painted hair.

🏠 **Porcupines.** Call your veterinarian. Pulling out or working out quills can be very painful for your Dachsie, and your vet may want to sedate the dog while he or she removes them.

🏠 **Skunks.** Soak your dog in tomato juice or vinegar, rubbing it deep into the coat; let it sit for a few minutes, then rinse it out. You may need to repeat the treatment several times. Joy dish soap also helps cut the smell (it works against the oil in the skunk's discharge). There are also commercial preparations on the market that work well, or you can make your own mixture of 1 quart peroxide, 1 teaspoon dish soap, and ¼ cup baking soda.

🏠 **Ticks.** Use rubber gloves or tweezers and, grasping the tick down at the skin, gently pull it out as you *slowly* twist it. Make sure to remove the head, too. If the head pulls off and remains embedded in your dog's skin, use the tweezers to remove the head and a little bit of skin where the tick was imbedded. A retained head will cause an infection! Burn the tick.

Trimming Toenails!

Letting your Dachsie's toenails grow too long is more than just a cosmetic problem; it can actually cause the dog foot pain and, over time, deform his feet. However, if you learn to trim the toenails while your Dachsie is young and the nails are soft, it won't become a problem.

Buy a pair of canine nail clippers at the groomer salon or at a pet-supply store. The best kind look like a pair of scissors with weird, curved blades. You will use them just like scissors, too.

Have your Dachsie lie down in your lap and roll him over so you can see his feet well. Give him some peanut butter to keep him occupied while you check out his feet. Taking one toe in your hand, look at the nail. Pull the hair away from the nail and hold it with your fingers. If the nail is clear or white, you will be able to see the pink quick inside. Trim the nail slightly beyond the quick so there is some leeway. If you cut the quick, your Dachsie will hurt, bleed, and be very upset!

Watch Out!

If you cut the quick of a toenail, scrape the nail along a bar of soap from the shower. The soft soap will clog the nail until the bleeding can clot. Keep the puppy on your lap with his foot up for a few minutes until the bleeding stops.

If your Dachsie has black nails, check all his toes. If he has one white nail, that will give you some guidelines as to where the quick is, and you can cut the black nails to slightly longer than that same spot. If there are no white nails, you will just have to practice and guess a little!

When you look at a toenail from the side, you will see it curves out and down. The last third of the nail is much narrower and comes to a point. It's always safe to trim off that last third of the nail. The quick doesn't extend into that part of the nail.

Keep toenail trimming sessions short and positive.

You might want to trim your Dachsie's nails weekly. Not only will this make sure he's used to the procedure, it will keep those little razor-sharp weapons trimmed! However, if your Dachsie really dislikes having his nails trimmed, don't try to do all four paws at the same time. Instead, trim a couple nails every night. This will keep temper tantrums to a minimum and show your Dachsie that it isn't as bad as he thought.

Bet You Didn't Know

When your Dachsie is standing still and upright on all four paws, his nails should not touch the floor. You may hear them clicking when he's running, but they should not touch the floor when standing. If they do, they need trimming.

Cleaning Your Dachsie's Ears

Cleaning your Dachsie's ears isn't a difficult procedure; nothing like trimming toenails. For one thing, there's no chance of making him bleed!

Grab a few cotton balls and a bottle of witch hazel or commercial canine ear cleaning solution (either are acceptable).

Wet a cotton ball with the witch hazel, alcohol, or solution and wring out most of the moisture. With your Dachsie on your lap and distracted by a lick of peanut butter, lift the ear flap and gently wipe the inside of the ear, making sure to get in all the folds and creases. Don't try to go deep within the ear; just clean what is easily reachable. If the ear is dirty, you may need two or three cotton balls.

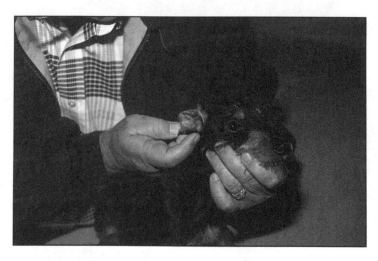

You must be able to care for your Dachsie, including cleaning his ears.

Brushing Those Pearly Whites

Dogs need their teeth brushed regularly for the same reasons we need to keep ours clean. A clean mouth and clean teeth are less likely to be diseased and cause diseases. In older dogs especially, dirty teeth and gums can lead to bacterial infections in other parts of the body, especially the heart. Teach your Dachsie to tolerate teeth brushing when he's young.

Get a very small child's toothbrush for your dog. Your veterinarian may have some canine toothpaste, or you can check at your local pet store. Or you can use baking soda.

Have your Dachsie lie down in your lap, and lift his lips with your fingers. Start gently rubbing the toothbrush up against the outside of his side teeth. He will probably try to chew on the brush and, if he does, take the brush away as you discourage him. Then try it again.

Watch Out!

Don't use toothpaste made for people on your Dachsie's teeth. Not all the ingredients are safe for dogs, and the taste is offensive to canines!

At first, brushing his teeth is going to take a lot of patience on your part. Obviously, you can't distract him with peanut butter as you can for many of the other grooming exercises. Instead, you need to be patient, do a few teeth at a time, and get him used to the procedure.

As with trimming toenails, sometimes it's better to do this as short session. Brush a few teeth, give him a break and then later, or the next day, brush some more.

The Daily Massage

It's important that you know your Dachsie's body very well. You need to know what is normal and what isn't. Your Dachsie often can't tell you when there's a problem. Sure, he can cry or limp when he hurts his paw, but how can he tell you when he has a lump on his side? He can't. As your Dachshund grows older and starts having the health problems common to old dogs, the daily massage will help you identify them before they turn into bigger problems.

If you make a habit of examining him each and every day, you can find anything out of the ordinary—anything that appears different. Often, the difference of a day or two can mean the difference between a minor problem and a major one.

The easiest and most enjoyable way to examine your Dachsie is to give him a massage. I like to do it in the evening when I'm watching television. I sit on the floor and invite my dog to lie in front of me between my legs. With her lying on her side, I start at her head and gently feel her muzzle. I peek in at her teeth, look at her nose and eyes, and rub the base of her ears as I look inside each ear. I massage her neck all around, trying to feel for lumps, bumps, burrs, foxtails, or anything else that might be a problem or different. I work down to the shoulders, the chest, down each front leg to the paws and check each paw. I continue this thorough massage and examination until I have gone over her entire body.

My dogs like this so much that by the time I'm done, they are as limp as dishrags, totally relaxed. Because of this relaxing effect, this massage is also good for calming a dog who is overexcited. It's always a wonderful bonding tool for newly adopted dogs.

The Least You Need to Know

- All Dachshunds need regular body care, no matter the coat type.
- Brushing, combing, and bathing your Dachsie should be regular chores.
- Trimming toenails, cleaning ears, and brushing teeth are part of the grooming routine.
- A daily massage helps you stay aware of your Dachsie's body and health.

Chapter 11

Food for the Tummy!

In This Chapter

- 🏠 All about doggy nutrition
- 🏠 The ins and outs of commercial dog food
- 🏠 Making your own food
- 🏠 Sizing up supplements and treats
- 🏠 Scheduling mealtimes

Your Dachsie depends on you for his food and good nutrition, and what you choose to feed him is vitally important. Poor nutrition could result in a lack of energy, poor health, and numerous health problems. In addition, some behavior problems can be the result of poor nutrition.

Your Dachsie needs a good food made from high-quality ingredients that satisfy all of his body's needs. Hopefully, it will also taste good (to him!) and won't break your bank account at the same time.

What Makes Food Good?

Everybody needs good nutrition. What that nutrition is depends on the body being nourished. Obviously, an *herbivorous* animal (such as a horse or sheep) will not have the same nutritional needs as a *carnivorous* animal (like a lion, tiger, or wolf). Dogs are scientifically considered carnivores, but all wild canine carnivores are known to eat other things as well. That's why your Dachsie may eat a ripe strawberry or a grape.

Nutritional needs don't remain the same throughout the animal's lifetime. They may change as the body changes, for example, from puppyhood to adulthood to old age. They may also change as environmental conditions change. Dogs living and working in colder climates will need more calories to keep their bodies warm than dogs working in a warmer climate will. Nutritional needs will change, too, as the activity levels change, because a hard-working dog will need the energy from food to perform his work.

___ **Dog Talk** ___
A **carnivore** eats meat, an **herbivore** eats plants, and an **omnivore** eats both plants and meat.

Your Dachsie needs a diet that fulfills all his nutrition needs so he can grow and remain healthy while having enough energy left for exercise and playtime. This good nutrition is made up of many things. Vitamins, minerals, proteins, amino acids, enzymes, fats, and carbohydrates are all necessary for good nutrition:

🏠 **Vitamins.** Organic compounds are necessary for life. Without these compounds, there could be no *metabolism* of food, no growth, and no reproduction, and there would be a total cessation of a thousand other bodily functions. Several vitamins, including A, D, E, and K, are fat soluble, which means the body can store them in fat. Other vitamins, including all the B complex vitamins and C, are water soluble. These are

___ **Dog Talk** ___
Metabolism is the process of converting food into chemical substances the body can use.

flushed out of the system daily in the urine and must be replenished through the foods consumed.

🏠 **Minerals.** These inorganic compounds are also necessary for life, although in much smaller amounts than vitamins and other nutrients. Essential minerals include calcium, phosphorus, copper, iron, and potassium, as well as several others. Minerals require a delicate balance for good health—some work only in the presence of others, and more of them isn't necessarily better.

Dachsie Wisdom

Often dogs (other than teething puppies) who eat dirt, chew on rocks, or chew on the stucco siding of the house do so because they crave minerals. If your Dachsie does any of these things, give him a mineral supplement or feed him a food with added minerals (look for minerals listed on the label).

🏠 **Protein.** Meat is good quality protein—beef, chicken, lamb, fish, or any other meat. Other parts of an animal's body are also good sources of protein, including skin, nails, claws, hooves, and blood, but these aren't as good (nutritionally speaking) as meat. Proteins are found in other sources, too, including eggs, dairy products, and some plants.

🏠 **Amino acids.** Amino acids are found in proteins—they are the building blocks of protein. In fact, during metabolism, proteins are broken down to form amino acids. They are necessary for many body functions, including growth and healing as well as for hormone, antibody, and enzyme production.

🏠 **Enzymes.** Every cell in the body contains enzymes. These are protein-based chemicals that cause biochemical reactions in the body and affect every stage of metabolism. Some enzymes must work with a partner, a co-enzyme that is often a vitamin, to cause the needed reaction or metabolism. Some enzymes are produced in the dog's body, while others are found in the food the dog eats.

🐾 **Fats.** Although they've gotten a lot of bad press lately, fats are a necessary part of good nutrition, especially for growing puppies and hard-working dogs. Fats are needed to metabolize the fat-soluble vitamins and to supply energy for activity.

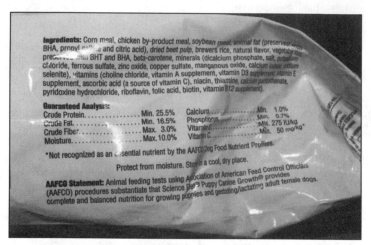

Know the food you are feeding your Dachsie; read the label and understand it.

Watch Out!

Some young dogs and puppies who eat high-carbohydrate foods show symptoms of hyperactivity. The symptoms will often disappear when they are given a diet lower in carbohydrates.

🐾 **Carbohydrates.** Sugars and starches are used primarily for fuel for the body. Your Dachsie's body runs on carbohydrates like your car runs on gasoline. Complex carbohydrates (potatoes, pasta, peas, grains, and rice) are intricate conglomerations of glucose (sugar) molecules.

Commercial Dog Foods Can Be Excellent

Commercial dog foods are designed to supply all your Dachsie's needs, including proteins, amino acids, enzymes, fats, carbohydrates, vitamins, and minerals. However, not all dog foods are created equal.

Dog foods are one area where you usually do get what you pay for. As a general rule, the more expensive dog foods are, the better quality they are. The less-expensive foods—especially the generic or plain label foods—are lesser-quality foods.

Instead of testing dog food by actually feeding dogs (called feeding trials), some companies might use only laboratory testing to determine the nutritional value of a food. Unfortunately, that testing doesn't measure the food as it is used or metabolized by the dog. Therefore, a food could test well but still not adequately nourish your dog. Foods that are tested by feeding trials will say so on the label of the dog food, or you can call the manufacturer—there is usually a phone number on the label—and ask.

Bet You Didn't Know

Many of the companies producing dog foods use feeding trials to test their foods and have fed, literally, generation after generation of dogs.

The quality of a dog food is also based on the quality of the ingredients. Grains grown in mineral-poor soils will have few minerals to pass on to the dog who consumes them. Poor-quality meats will be less able to nourish the dog. Less-expensive foods typically contain inexpensive and less-nourishing grains and less of the more expensive meats. Again, the dog's nutrition can, and often will, suffer.

Many dog owners are also concerned about many of the preservatives, artificial flavorings, and additives in many dog foods. Some of these additives are of questionable nutritional value. If you are concerned about a particular additive or ingredient, call your veterinarian and the manufacturer of the food. Find out what they each say about that ingredient.

Bet You Didn't Know

Symptoms of inadequate nutrition may include some or all of the following: flaky skin, dull coat, brittle nails, less than normal energy for work or play, poor stamina, and insatiable appetite. In addition, the dog may eat strange things, including rocks, dirt, stucco off the side of the house, or wood.

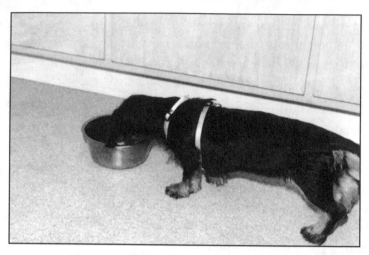

Your dog's health depends on good-quality food.

Reading the Label

The label on each bag (or can) of dog food will tell you a lot about that particular food. One section of the label lists the percentages of nutrients. Most puppies and hard-working dogs will thrive on a food that contains about 28 percent protein and 8 percent fat; while inactive dogs may do better with 24 percent protein and 6 percent fat.

The label will also tell you the food's ingredients. Ingredients are listed in order of amounts contained. Therefore, if beef is listed first, followed by rice, corn, and wheat, you'll know that there is more beef in the food than there is rice and there is more rice than corn. However, this listing can be deceptive. You might see wheat middlings, wheat germ, and wheat bran all listed after the meat ingredient. Because they are listed after the meat, does that mean there is more meat than wheat? Not necessarily. There might be more meat than wheat middlings, or more meat than wheat germ. But if all

Dachsie Wisdom

Ingredients are even more important if your dog develops allergies. Many dogs are allergic to wheat, for example, and those dog owners must read the labels very carefully.

the wheat is added together, there might very well be more wheat than meat. You need to read the label carefully so you know exactly what you're feeding your dog.

Are Preservatives Safe?

Most commercial dog foods are preserved with something—chemical or natural—to extend the food's shelf life. Unfortunately, some preservatives have been linked with health problems. The most controversial preservative currently used in dog foods is ethoxyquin, a chemical that prevents the fats in foods from becoming rancid and the vitamins from losing their potency. Ethoxyquin is approved by the Food and Drug Administration for use in human foods, but it has come under criticism from the general public. It has been alleged that ethoxyquin causes cancer and kidney, liver, and thyroid problems. However, none of these claims have been proven.

If you are concerned about ethoxyquin or any other chemical preservatives, look for a food preserved with tocopherols. These antioxidants are naturally occurring compounds of vitamins C and E. Just be aware that tocopherols have a very short shelf life; make sure to check the expiration date on the food.

Different Forms of Food

Dog food is most often available in three basic types: dry kibble, canned, and semi-moist.

Dry, kibbled foods come in a bag and usually contain grains and meats. Dry foods have a good shelf life, and most dogs eat them quite readily. They are usually very affordable; some more so than others.

Canned foods are mostly meats (chunks or slices of meat) or meat recipes (processed meat with other ingredients). These foods have a high moisture content. They have a long shelf life in the can, but once the can is opened they must be used right away. Canned foods are very palatable to dogs and are much more expensive than dry foods.

Semi-moist foods have a higher moisture content than dry kibble foods but not as high as canned foods. They contain a lot of sugar and salt as well as artificial colorings. The ingredients can vary significantly, so it's important to read the label to see what the food contains. Many treats are semi-moist.

In addition to the three basic types of foods, there are also frozen foods—these are usually meat-based with some grains or vegetables—and there are some dehydrated foods—again, mostly meat-based. Some dog owners even like to feed human food to their dogs, cooking for them on a daily basis.

Dachsie Wisdom

Nutrition is a very complex subject, and I could write an entire book about reading labels and selecting the right food for your dog. In fact, I did! It's called *The Consumer's Guide to Dog Food* (Howell Book House, 1996).

So what kind of food should you feed your Dachsie? Most veterinarians recommend dry foods because they have a longer shelf life, are easy to keep, are reasonably priced, and because the chewing action required to eat the hard kibble helps keep the dog's teeth clean. However, that doesn't mean the other foods are bad or of lesser quality. Ultimately, the choice is yours.

Choosing the Right Commercial Food

Choosing the right food for your dog can be difficult. Here are some suggestions to help you decide:

🏠 Read the ingredients. Is there a good variety of foods? Are there complete and incomplete proteins? Is there a selection of carbohydrates and fats? What about additives and preservatives? Do you understand what they are and why they are in the food?

🏠 Look at the nutritional information to find the protein and fat percentages. Are you comfortable with those levels?

🏠 Again, read the nutritional information to determine whether the food will supply the needed calories for your dog without supplying too much.

🏠 If you have any questions about the food, talk to your veterinarian and call the food manufacturer.

After your dog has been eating the food for four to six weeks, evaluate the results. This is the food's final test and will help you decide whether or not this is the right food for your dog.

🏠 If your Dachsie is a puppy, is he growing well?

🏠 How is your dog's weight? Is he too skinny? Is he too fat?

🏠 How is your Dachsie's coat? It should be shiny and soft, with no oily feel and no doggy odor.

🏠 What is your Dachsie's energy level like? Does he have enough energy for work and play? Does he have too much energy? Does he act hyperactive? He should have plenty of energy for work and play without bouncing off the walls.

🏠 Does he act starved or always hungry? Often those dogs whose bodies are missing vital nutrients will chew on everything and will act starved even though they are eating regularly.

Are Home-Cooked Meals Okay?

Some Dachsie owners, especially those concerned about the ingredients in commercial dog foods, prefer to cook for their dog. With home-cooked meals, you have a little more control over exactly what goes into your dog's food.

Because they aren't formulated by experts and haven't been tested, home-cooked meals can be risky to your dog's nutritional health. However, many people feed their dogs home-cooked meals quite successfully.

The key to making a homemade diet work is using a variety of ingredients to make sure the dog is receiving all the necessary amino acids and enzymes, as well as his required vitamins and minerals.

Basic Home-Cooked Diet

Try the following recipe for a home-cooked maintenance diet for dogs who have no known food allergies. The amount fed each day will vary depending on your Dachsie's weight, weight loss or weight gain, activity level, and energy needs.

Mix together in a big bowl:

1 lb. ground meat (chicken, turkey, or lamb), cooked and drained of most of the fat

2 cups cooked sweet potato, chopped

½ cup barley, cooked and mashed

½ cup oatmeal, cooked

½ cup raw carrots, grated

½ cup raw green vegetables (no lettuce), finely chopped

2 TB. olive oil

2 TB. garlic, minced or mashed

Store in the refrigerator in a covered bowl, or divide into daily servings and store in the freezer. Thaw one day's serving at a time.

Dachsie Wisdom

A **supplement** is anything added to the food or to the dog's diet. Commercial vitamins, herbal remedies, and additional foods are all examples of supplements.

When serving, add the following:

1 TB. yogurt with live active cultures

1 multi-vitamin/mineral dog *supplement*

Pinch kelp

Active Dog Home-Cooked Diet

This home-cooked diet is for active dogs, dogs under stress, or pregnant or lactating bitches.

Mix together in a large bowl:

1 lb. ground meat, cooked; do not drain off the fat

4 large hardboiled eggs, shelled and crumbled

2 cups cooked sweet potato, chopped

1 cup cooked oatmeal

1 large russet or red potato, cooked and mashed

¼ cup wheat germ (as long as dog is not allergic to wheat)

½ cup raw carrots, grated

½ cup green vegetables, finely chopped

2 TB. olive oil

2 TB. garlic, minced or mashed

Store in refrigerator in a covered bowl or divide into daily servings and freeze; thawing servings one day at a time.

When serving, add the following:

1 TB. yogurt with live active cultures

Dash dry powdered milk

Dash brewer's yeast

Pinch kelp

1 vitamin/mineral dog supplement

Hypoallergenic Diet

This diet is for dogs allergic to meats or grains and grain products.

Mix together in a large bowl:

5 large potatoes (russet or sweet), cooked and mashed

3 eggs, hardboiled, shelled and crumbled

1 cup green vegetables, finely chopped or grated

1 cup cooked beans (not green beans), finely chopped or mashed

½ cup carrots, grated

2 TB. olive oil

1 TB. garlic, minced

Store in covered bowl in refrigerator or divide into daily servings and freeze.

Add when serving:

1 TB. yogurt with live active cultures

1 vitamin/mineral supplement

Pinch kelp

When Changing Diets

If you decide to change from a dry kibble commercial food diet to a home-cooked diet, do so very slowly over a two- to three-week period. A home-cooked diet is very different, and if you change foods too quickly, your dog might suffer from severe gastrointestinal upset.

Watch Out!
Dry kibble foods help keep your Dachsie's teeth clean by the scraping action that occurs when he's chewing. A home-cooked diet will not do this, so you will have to work harder and be more meticulous about keeping his teeth clean.

Cook some of the new diet and begin adding it to your Dachsie's old food a tablespoon at a time, daily, for several days.

Then, make his food ⅓ the new diet and ⅔ the old food for a week. Then make it ⅓ the old food and ⅔ the new food. If he is doing okay and his stools are firm, go ahead and switch him completely to the new diet.

Water is necessary for good health. Make sure it is always available.

What About Supplements?

Most commercial dog foods state on the label that the food provides complete and balanced nutrition—that means no supplementation is needed. However, many nutritional experts who don't work in the commercial dog food industry say that such statements don't take into account that every dog is different and every dog's nutritional needs are different. Supplements, nutritionists argue, can make the difference between good nutrition and better nutrition.

Some supplements that can improve your Dachsie's nutrition and not cause a nutritional imbalance might include the following:

🏠 **Yogurt.** A good nutritious food on its own and a good source of protein, amino acids, and fat, yogurt with live active cultures adds beneficial bacteria to the digestive tract. Add no more than 1 heaping teaspoon per day for a Dachsie.

🏠 **Brewer's yeast.** This is an excellent source of B vitamins and minerals, including the essential trace minerals chromium and selenium, and is a good nutritious food on its own. Add no more than 1 teaspoon or according to manufacturer's directions.

🏠 **Eggs.** Cooked only (raw egg yolks interfere with vitamin B absorption and have been associated with salmonella poisonings), eggs are excellent sources of proteins, a variety of vitamins, minerals, and amino acids. Give your Dachsie one to three cooked eggs per week.

> **Watch Out!**
> Too much supplementation can upset the nutritional balance of the previously balanced commercial food. Supplement carefully and wisely. When in doubt, talk to your veterinarian, the dog food company, and the makers of the supplement and then balance all their recommendations.

🏠 **Kelp.** Kelp is a good source of iodine, calcium, potassium, and other minerals and essential trace elements. Use according to manufacturer's directions.

When adding supplements to your Dachsie's food, make sure you add small amounts so the total of supplements will not add up to more than 10 percent of the dog's daily diet. Any more than this could upset the nutritional balance of the commercial food.

Are Treats Okay?

Treats are fine as long as your Dachsie doesn't get too many. The general rule of thumb is that anything added to the diet—including supplements and treats—should not total more than 10 percent of the diet. Therefore, if you use treats for training, be aware of how many you are giving and hand them out carefully.

Choose treats that your Dachsie likes but that are also good food. If you give your dog junk food treats (loaded with sugar, food colorings, and other garbage), they will negatively affect his total diet. Instead, read the labels on the treats just as you do his regular food, and choose treats that have better ingredients.

When Should Your Dachsie Eat?

Most young puppies need to eat two to three times per day. A big morning meal, a small lunch, and a big evening meal usually suit 8- to 12-week-old puppies just fine. By 12 weeks of age, most puppies will be able to drop the lunch meal and do quite well with just morning and evening meals.

Dachsie Wisdom
If your Dachsie is healthy and growing well, don't force him to eat more than he wants.

How Much Is Enough?

The label on your Dachsie's food will state feeding recommendations. If your dog eats that much, he will be getting all of the needed nutrition available from that food. However, those directions are just the beginning; every dog will have different dietary needs depending on the individual dog's body metabolism, activity level, and personality. A 10-pound mini Dachsie who is active and hard working will need more calories from his food than another 10-pound mini Dachsie who is a little more laid back and relaxed.

Adjust your feeding amounts according to how your dog is doing. If he is thin and always seems hungry, give him more food. If some padding appears over his ribs and he is looking a little chubby, cut back on the food a little bit. Add more when your dog is working hard, and cut back when things are quiet.

No Free-Feeding!

Do not leave food out for your Dachsie to nibble on all day. This is called free-feeding and is not recommended for several reasons.

First, if your dog happens to get sick, the first questions the veterinarian will ask are, "How is your dog's appetite?" and "How did he eat this morning?" If the dog eats sporadically throughout the day rather than at specific times, you won't be able to answer those questions.

In addition, housetraining a puppy is much easier when the puppy eats at specific times. You know that he will need to go outside after every meal. If those meals are at set times, you know when to take him outside. However, if the puppy snacks all day, when should you take him out? It's much more difficult to tell.

Feeding at set times also helps develop the proper relationship between you and your dog. As the giver of the food at each mealtime, you assume a very important position in your dog's life. After all, to the dog, food is survival.

Bet You Didn't Know

If your dog is hesitant about a particular family member, have that person feed the dog. This will help change how that person is viewed in the dog's eyes.

Food that is set out for free-feeding is also easily spoiled. Ants, flies, and other insects can soil it; rodents can visit it; and heat or water can spoil it.

The Least You Need to Know

- A good-quality food is important to your dog's good health.

- You get what you pay for with dog foods. Generally the more expensive foods are better quality.

- Dog food labels will tell you a lot about the food, including ingredients, nutritional value, and the preservatives used.

- Free-feeding is not a good idea; feed your Dachsie on a regular schedule.

Chapter 12

Pay Attention to These Health Concerns

In This Chapter

- 🏠 Bugs that can pester your Dachsie
- 🏠 Internal parasites to watch out for
- 🏠 Dangerous Dachsie diseases
- 🏠 Dachsie back needs

Dachsies are, as a breed, very healthy. Luckily, they aren't prone to many genetic health threats—although there are a few you should know about. Also, all Dachsie owners need to be aware of potential problems with that sometimes-fragile Dachsie back. In addition to problems Dachsies are especially prone to, this chapter discusses other health problems that all dogs are susceptible to.

You need to be able to identify health threats and know how to prevent them. Of course, you also need to know what to do should your Dachsie be afflicted.

Is Something Bugging You?: The Nature of External Parasites

Most of us cringe at the thought of insects living on us or any members of our family—including our dog! The idea of bugs in our house grosses me out, and I'm sure it does you, too. We have been raised with the idea that insects in the home symbolize dirt, poor housekeeping, ignorance, or poverty. However, none of those things are necessarily true! There are insects in our homes all the time—we just don't see most of them! Experts tell us there are dust mites in our carpets and drapes; bed bugs and mites in our mattresses; spiders behind the pictures on the wall … and that's not even the half of it!

The *parasites* sometimes found on our pets—fleas, ticks, and mites—are uniquely suited to bug them. Fleas that live on dogs are not the same as fleas that live on other animals, such as horses, monkeys, or bats, and mites that thrive on dogs are not the same as the mites that live with (and on!) humans. Now that's not to say that these insects won't take a nibble out of you; often they will. It's just that they would prefer to munch on your dog instead!

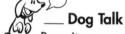

Dog Talk

Parasites are creatures that live off another creature, either internally or externally.

Bet You Didn't Know

Most flea circuses (remember those?) never contained any live fleas. The so-called fleas were either dead and glued into place or were so small they were invisible!

Fleas, ticks, and mites have a long history of destruction. Fleas have been blamed for innumerable plagues throughout history, including the bubonic plague that decimated Europe hundreds of years ago. Today, these are still pests, and they can still threaten your dog's comfort and health, although we have a much better arsenal at our fingertips to combat them.

Fleas

A flea is a small, slightly crescent shaped, six-legged insect with a big abdomen and a small head. It is a tremendous jumper and is flat sided so it can slip through hair with ease. When caught, it will pop under or between your fingernails like a tiny balloon. If that sounds gross, you obviously haven't dealt with too many fleas! Fleas cause dogs so much torment, it can be very satisfying to pop the little pests!

Fleas live by biting your Dachsie, taking a drop or two of blood each time they bite. A heavy infestation can actually cause anemia from the blood loss, especially for small, young puppies.

Many dogs are so allergic to flea bites, the poor dogs will scratch, dig, and chew themselves raw. An allergic Dachsie could end up with flea bite dermatitis or open sores which could then develop secondary infections.

Fleas are also the intermediate host for tapeworms, which will be discussed later in this chapter. If your Dachsie has fleas and, during chewing, swallows an infected flea, the dog can become infested with tapeworms. Fleas can also carry human diseases, including bubonic plague. Obviously, these pests are more than simply annoying to you and your dog, they are also a very real health threat.

> **Dachsie Wisdom**
> Think about the worst bug bite you've ever had, then multiply it thousands of times! That's what a flea-infested allergic dog feels like!

Luckily, in the past few years several products have been introduced to make flea control easier and safer. In past years, insecticides and pesticides were the only available products, and you had to use those with caution. If you weren't careful, you could easily end up poisoning yourself and your dog before you killed off all the fleas.

Some new options include the following:

🏠 **Systemic products.** Your dog swallows a pill that transmits a chemical throughout the body. When the flea bites the dog, it picks up this chemical. The chemical prevents the flea's eggs from developing and, hence, the insect population dies off.

🏠 **Insect growth regulators (IGRs).** These products stop the immature flea from developing or maturing. It then cannot reproduce.

🏠 **Systemic topical treatments.** These products are applied to your dog's skin, usually between the shoulder blades, and the product is absorbed into the dog's system. Depending upon the product used, the flea (and tick) is either killed when it bites the dog or its reproduction cycle is disrupted.

To control fleas, you must hit them in three ways: on the dog, in your house, and in your yard. Leave out any one of the three, and your control efforts will not be successful. However, with the new products available, flea control is now possible, whereas a few years ago, the battle was ongoing with the fleas often winning!

Some relatively safe control methods might include the following:

🏠 **In the yard.** Use a spray designed for outside use that contains an IGR. Use it repeatedly according to directions.

🏠 **In the house.** Use a spray for inside use with an IGR. If your house is infested, use a spray with a quick kill ingredient as well as an IGR. Use according to directions.

🏠 **On the dog.** Use a systemic product such as Program or Sentinel. Do not use insecticides on the dog at the same time as flea collars, unless the label on both products specifies that it is safe to do so.

Fleas may seem tiny and inconsequential, but they can be dangerous to your Dachsie's health.

Some owners prefer to use more natural products to control fleas. Some of those products include feeding garlic, yeast, B complex vitamins, and other combinations of similar products. These will not hurt the dog when given in appropriate dosages; however, they are usually not entirely effective in controlling fleas by themselves. They can, of course, be used in conjunction with other flea control methods.

Watch Out!
Mixing different flea control products can be deadly. Don't use a flea spray as well as a flea collar, for example. Read the labels carefully, and follow the directions.

Watch Out!
Be careful using pennyroyal or eucalyptus. The oil from each is poisonous if ingested by the dog.

Cedar or eucalyptus bedding or pennyroyal are also supposed to help repel fleas, especially in the dog's bedding. They can also help with flea control, but again are not usually effective by themselves.

Ticks

Ticks are eight-legged, oblong insects with a head that embeds into the skin. Ticks feed on the host's blood and, when engorged, will drop off. Ticks, like fleas, are carriers of human diseases. In the western North America, ticks carry Rocky Mountain spotted fever, an acutely infectious disease characterized by muscular pains, high fevers, and skin eruptions.

Dachsie Wisdom
Ask your veterinarian whether Lyme disease is a problem in your area. If it is, there is a Lyme disease vaccine. Ask your vet whether he recommends it.

Ticks are also carriers of Lyme disease, which affects dogs as well as people. A lingering fever and joint pain (sometimes quite severe) are characteristics of this disease.

Although some flea products are partially effective on ticks, they are rarely totally effective at killing or keeping ticks off your dog. During tick season (spring and summer), you will have to examine your dog daily and remove each and every tick. Check your dog all over, but pay especially close attention to ticks' favorite spots: behind or in the ears, in the armpit area of the front legs, and around the neck.

Never remove a tick with your bare fingers. Use tweezers or wear rubber gloves. Grab down close to the skin, and pull gently but firmly with a slow twisting motion. Don't flush the tick; it will survive its trip downstream. Instead, burn it to kill it. Put a little antibiotic ointment on the wound where the tick was embedded.

Mange Mites

Most people usually associate mange with stray dogs who have no one to care for them. This isn't necessarily so. Many well-loved dogs have come down with mange one way or another.

Sarcoptic mange is contagious to people and other pets. Its primary symptoms include red welts, and the dog will be scratching continuously. Sarcoptic mange usually reacts well to treatment.

Demodectic mange is not as easily transmitted to people or other pets and shows up with bald patches, usually first on the dog's face, and there may not be any scratching or itching. Demodectic mange often appears in young dogs (especially at puberty) and will usually clear up with treatment. However, in older dogs, treatment can be long and drawn out and is sometimes not effective at all.

Watch Out!

Mange mite infestations (even apparently minor ones) should always be seen and treated by a veterinarian. The mites can only be seen under a microscope, and the vet will do a scraping to find them.

Ringworm

Ringworm isn't really a worm at all; it's a contagious fungus that infests the skin and causes ring-shape (round) scaly, itchy spots. These round spots are the trademark identification of ringworm.

Ringworm is spread on contact—perhaps with an infested cat, squirrel, rabbit, or another dog. Infection usually responds well to treatment, but care must be taken to follow the treatment plan according to directions as set up by your veterinarian because this is very, very contagious to people and other pets.

And You Thought Fleas Were Bad!: Internal Parasites

Unlike external parasites, which you can usually see and, thus, treat early, internal parasites aren't easily seen, and you may not be able to tell if your dog has them. He could have internal parasites for quite a while before you see any signs of poor health.

Most internal parasites can be detected by taking a small piece of your dog's stool to the veterinarian's office. The stool will be prepared and then examined under a microscope, which will reveal the parasites themselves or their eggs or larvae, and your vet can prescribe appropriate treatment. After treatment, your vet will ask you to bring in another stool sample—usually in two to three weeks—to make sure the treatment was effective.

> **Watch Out!**
> Generic, over-the-counter wormers are usually not recommended, as not all internal parasites react or are controlled by these generic medications.

Roundworms

Roundworms are long white worms that are fairly common in puppies, although they can also be found in adult dogs and humans as well as other animals.

Although you never want to ignore it, a roundworm infestation in an adult dog isn't always dangerous, especially a light infestation. However, a heavy infestation can threaten a dog's health. A young puppy with roundworms will not thrive and will appear thin, with a dull coat and a pot belly. All puppies must be treated for roundworms.

> **Bet You Didn't Know**
> Roundworm eggs can be picked up via the feces; your dog should be discouraged from sniffing other dogs' feces.

If your dog has a roundworm infection, you will often see worms in the stool. They also can be detected by your veterinarian through a fecal analysis.

Because roundworm eggs can be picked up via the feces, discourage your dog from sniffing other dogs' feces. Good sanitation also is important to prevent an infestation, and feces should be picked up and disposed of daily.

Hookworms

Hookworms are parasites that live in the small intestine, where they attach to the intestinal wall and suck blood. When they detach and move to a new location, the old wound continues to bleed for a period of time, causing bloody diarrhea, which is often a symptom of a hookworm infestation.

Hookworm eggs are passed through the feces and are either picked up from the stools, as with roundworms, or if conditions are right, they will hatch in the soil and the larvae will attach themselves to the feet of their new host. They burrow into the skin of the feet (human or canine), after which they migrate to the intestinal tract where the cycle then repeats itself.

The eggs can be detected in a fecal analysis. Treatment often needs to be repeated two or more times before finally ridding the host of the parasites. Good sanitation is necessary to prevent a reinfestation.

Watch Out!
People can pick up hookworms by walking barefoot in infected soil. Infestations are very common in the sunbelt states.

Tapeworms

Tapeworms are another parasite that lives in the intestinal tract and attaches to the wall to absorb nutrients. They grow by creating new segments. Usually, the first sign of an infestation is small ricelike segments found around the dog's rectum or in its stool.

Tapeworms are acquired when the dog eats an infected flea, the intermediate host. The flea may be on the dog or may be swallowed when the dog catches a squirrel or a mouse. A good flea control program is the best way to prevent a tapeworm infestation. Infestations can be treated with oral medications or injections.

Whipworms

These worms live in the large intestine where they feed on blood. The eggs are passed in the feces and can live in the soil for a long time—even years. A dog who eats the fresh spring grass or buries his bone in the infected soil can pick up eggs.

Heavy infestations can cause diarrhea and can even be fatal; infested dogs will appear thin and anemic, with a poor coat. Whipworms are not as easily detected through fecal analysis, as these worms do not shed eggs in the stools as frequently as do roundworms and hookworms. Several stool samples may need to be checked to be certain. Once diagnosed, infestations are treatable.

> **Watch Out!**
> If you garden, you can pick up eggs under your fingernails, infecting yourself when you touch your face.

Heartworms

Heartworms, a parasite that lives in the upper heart and greater pulmonary arteries, damage blood vessel walls. Large numbers of worms can also impede blood flow in the heart and vessels. Poor circulation results, which, in turn, damages other body functions. Eventually, the heart fails, and the dog dies.

The adult worms produce thousands of tiny worms known as microfilariae. These circulate throughout the bloodstream until they are picked up by mosquitoes; the intermediate host. The microfilariae continue to develop in the mosquito and can be transferred to another dog when that mosquito bites it.

Dogs infested with heartworm can be treated when the infestation is in its early stages; however, heavy infestations are difficult to treat as the treatment itself is risky. Fortunately, preventive medications are available, easy to administer, and very effective. Talk to your veterinarian about heartworm preventives and whether heartworm has been found in your area. Yearly or biannual blood tests to check for heartworm are recommended in areas where heartworm is prevalent.

Giardiasis

The parasitic protozoa, *Giardia*, is common in wild animals. If you and your dog go camping or hiking and take a drink from a clear mountain stream, you can both ingest giardia and end up with a case of giardiasis. Diarrhea is one of the first symptoms, and dehydration, nausea, and a lack of energy follow quickly.

It's treated with antiprotozoan drugs. And if you can't keep your dog from drinking out of puddles and streams, it's impossible to absolutely prevent.

 **Dachsie Wisdom**

If you or your dog come home from a camping trip feeling ill, tell your physician or veterinarian where you've been.

Coccidiosis

Coccidiosis is another parasitic protozoa, but this one is often carried by birds and rabbits. Symptoms include coughing, a runny nose, eye discharge, and diarrhea. It can be diagnosed through a fecal analysis be treated with antiprotozoan drugs.

Bet You Didn't Know

If you have a birdfeeder in your backyard, make sure the area under the feeder is fenced off so your Dachsie can't eat fallen seeds (she will eat them!) and in the process also pick up bird feces and, possibly, coccidiosis.

Dangerous Doggy Diseases

Although many of the dangerous diseases that used to kill thousands of dogs every year are now controllable by vaccinations, it's important to know why your Dachsie needs these vaccines. Because vaccinations have reduced the number of illnesses and deaths, we sometimes get complacent and assume these diseases are no longer a threat. In fact, the diseases have not been eradicated, they are simply reduced in number because of the vaccinations.

Unfortunately, some puppies and dogs—even those who have been vaccinated—will still get sick. Perhaps the dog's immune system wasn't functioning properly, the virus causing the disease mutated, or the vaccine itself was ineffective. We see virus mutations every year with the human flu or influenza viruses; the same thing can and does happen with viruses infecting dogs.

Distemper

Distemper is a contagious viral disease that used to kill thousands of dogs each year. Fortunately, vaccines are now available that should be able to prevent this disease (and for the most part do), but some dogs still die from it.

Dogs with distemper have a fever, are weak or depressed, have a discharge from the eyes and nose, cough, vomit, and have diarrhea. Many show neurological symptoms also, such as staggering and lack of coordination. The virus is passed through the saliva, urine, and feces. Most infected dogs die.

Distemper vaccination usually prevents the disease; however, vaccines work by stimulating the immune system. If the immune system is threatened or if the puppy does not receive the complete series of vaccines, he may not be adequately protected.

Infectious Canine Hepatitis

Infectious canine hepatitis is another highly contagious viral disease. It primarily attacks the liver but can also damage the kidneys. It is not related to the human forms of hepatitis. The virus is spread through the saliva, mucus, urine, and feces. Initial symptoms include depression, vomiting, abdominal pain, fever, and jaundice.

Mild cases can be treated, but the mortality rate is very high. Vaccinations can prevent this disease.

Coronavirus

Coronavirus is rarely fatal for adult dogs, but it can be very dangerous for puppies. Symptoms include vomiting and loose, watery diarrhea. The virus is shed in the stools. Dehydration from the diarrhea and vomiting is the primary danger for puppies. Vaccinations can prevent this virus.

Parvovirus

Commonly called parvo, parvovirus is a terrible killer of puppies. It attacks the inner lining of the intestines, causing bloody diarrhea. This diarrhea has a very distinctive smell that veterinarians and breeders who have dealt with the disease quickly learn to recognize. In young puppies, the disease also attacks the heart, causing death, often with no other symptoms. The virus replicates very quickly, and dehydration can lead to shock and death within a matter of hours.

The vaccination for parvo is usually effective, although this virus has been known to mutate, rending the vaccine useless.

Bet You Didn't Know
The parvovirus vaccine is often given in conjunction with other vaccines; however, many vets and breeders feel that it should be given alone for the best results.

Leptospirosis

Leptospirosis is caused by bacteria, rather than a virus, and is passed in the urine. The bacteria attacks the kidneys, causing kidney failure. Symptoms include fever, loss of appetite, possible diarrhea, and jaundice. Antibiotics can sometimes treat the disease, but some dogs die, primarily due to the tremendous damage the disease causes.

Watch Out!
Some Dachsies have a sensitivity to leptospirosis vaccinations. Reactions might include swelling and a rash (or hives) appearing shortly after the vaccination is given. If your Dachsie has had this reaction in the past, inform your veterinarian; she might want to administer an antihistamine prior to the vaccination in the future.

Vaccinations will usually prevent leptospirosis, but care must be taken (through quarantining the sick dog, washing hands well with antibacterial soap, and following the vet's guidelines) to not spread this highly contagious disease, which can spread to people and other dogs.

Kennel Cough

Tracheobronchitis, adenovirus, and parainfluenza are a few of the diseases commonly referred to as kennel cough or canine cough. All three cause significant coughing, sometimes with a fever, sometimes without. Most healthy adult dogs can recuperate from these without veterinary care; however, young puppies and older dogs need careful monitoring, as a secondary respiratory infection can occur. In some cases, pneumonia develops.

Vaccinations usually prevent these diseases; however, viruses can and do mutate and often well-vaccinated dogs will still come down with some form of kennel cough. What strain or variety is often unknown.

Bet You Didn't Know _____

Kennel cough is actually a syndrome as opposed to a discrete disease, and it has multiple causes. It's similar to how we say we have a "cold" when we exhibit certain symptoms, even though a wide variety of viruses and bacteria may be involved. Tracheobronchitis, adenovirus, and parainfluenza are often called kennel cough because the dog may come down with it after being at a boarding kennel; however, as long as the kennel requires up-to-date vaccines, don't blame the kennel if your dog catches it. The virus that causes kennel cough mutates and changes, is transmitted through coughing, and can be spread anywhere dogs congregate.

Bordetella Bronchiseptica

Bordetella is another coughing disorder, this one caused by bacteria, that is also often called kennel cough or canine cough. The bacteria is spread through mucus and saliva, often through droplets coughed out by an affected dog. A vaccination can prevent this disease.

Rabies

The rabies virus is carried by infected wildlife and is highly contagious. It is transmitted in the salvia, either through a break in the skin or by a bite. It is always fatal.

Vaccines, however, have been very effective in preventing the disease, and rabies vaccines are required by law prior to obtaining a dog license.

Watch Out! _____
Never let your Dachsie chase or play with a wild animal that is acting abnormal. Bats, skunks, and raccoons, especially, have been known to carry rabies.

Oh, That Dachshund Back!

The Dachshund's long back is the breed's trademark, along with the short legs and feisty attitude. Unfortunately, that long back is also a trademark for a damaged back. The long back and short legs make the Dachsie extremely susceptible to injury. When that is combined with the breed's tendency to have thinner and more fragile spinal discs … well, it's an injury waiting to happen.

Dachsies usually injure their back when they are doing something, such as jumping off the sofa or out of the car, that causes them to land with a jolt. Injuries may also happen when the dog is twisting, such as to catch a ball. The jolt or twist puts pressure on a disc (or two or three) and the disc ruptures, producing a leak that puts pressure on the spinal cord. In some cases, the disc may actually burst out of its covering, putting severe pressure on the spinal cord.

Pressure on the spinal cord results in pain, usually severe pain. However, as if pain weren't enough damage, excess pressure on the spinal cord can also cut off blood supply; if that blood supply is not regained very, very quickly, the spinal cord can die, causing permanent paralysis.

If you suspect your Dachsie has injured his back, even slightly, call your vet. Even an injury that appears to be minor may cause lasting damage. Your vet may discuss several treatment options with you, depending on the type of injury and its severity. Surgery is usually very effective when undertaken right away—within 24 hours of the injury. If surgery is not an option, bed rest (or crate rest) for several weeks may also be recommended.

Watch Out!
Don't try to diagnose and treat your Dachsie's back problems yourself. Your dog's mobility and life may depend on prompt, professional treatment.

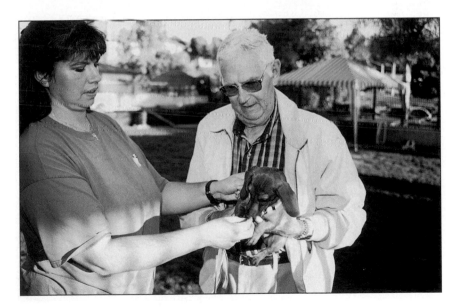

A well-behaved Dachsie can be your best friend.

Dachsies come in many colors and coats.

Dachsies like to play with people …

… as much as they like to play with other dogs.

Trim your Dachsie's nails regularly.

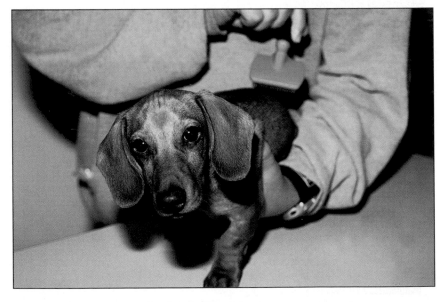

Daily brushing keeps your Dachsie looking smart.

A well-socialized Dachsie won't be afraid of other dogs or strangers.

A few simple preventative measures will keep your Dachsie out of the trash and out of trouble.

It takes time to train your Dachsie, but the effort will be worth it.

Make sure your Dachsie has a few toys to play with.

A healthy, well-behaved Dachsie is irresistible.

Genetic, Congenital, and Other Health Problems

When a Dachsie inherits a health problem from her ancestors, it's called a genetic health problem. Either the mother or father (or both) had the gene causing the problem, or one or both were carriers of the gene. Although scientists have made great progress in understanding the nature of how diseases are passed through genes, they don't yet fully understand the process.

A healthy Dachshund looks bright and alert.

Congenital health problems are present at birth but are not always hereditary; many times the cause is unknown. Identifying which health problems are genetic or congenital is also the subject of much study and debate. For example, Distichiasis, a condition caused by a double row of eye lashes, can severely irritate your Dachsie and eventually—if untreated—cause blindness. This condition appears to be inherited; however, that has yet to be proven. It is easy to assign blame (such as saying the breeder did not adequately screen the dogs bred to produce an affected puppy); however, it is much more difficult to scientifically prove the cause.

> **Dog Talk**
> **Congenital health problems** are present at birth and are also called birth defects.

Because many of these health threats are still being investigated and the causes are not yet proven, I will not lay blame. Instead, the health threats themselves will be discussed. With all these health threats, should you suspect a problem, contact your veterinarian for appropriate diagnosis and, if needed, treatment.

The Eyes

The beautiful merle coloring so many people associate with dapple Dachshunds has some hidden dangers within it. The merle gene has associated with it the potential for eye and ear defects. When a dapple bitch and a dapple dog are bred, the odds are that at least one out of four puppies (called double dapples) will have either a vision or hearing defect of some kind. If there is a dapple-to-dapple breeding in the background of either the sire (the puppies' father) or the dam (the puppies' mother), the odds of defects are increased even more. Many breeders will not breed dapples to dapples for this reason.

The homozygous merle eye defect, as the problems resulting from breeding two dogs with the merle gene are called, can include microphthalmia (abnormally small eyes), subluxated pupils (pupils off center in the iris), iris colobomas (holes in the iris), or optic disc colobomas (irregularities in the optic disc). Often, these defects are accompanied by irregular markings, including excess white on the dog's head, especially surrounding the eyes or ears.

Other eye defects that may appear in Dachsies include the following:

- **Glaucoma.** As with people, this refers to increased pressure within the eyeball.

- **Progressive retinal atrophy (PRA).** The retina deteriorates and vision decreases, leading to blindness. Lesions can be detected on the retina.

- **Optic nerve hypoplasia.** The optic nerve has failed to develop properly. The dogs affected are visually impaired.

- **Distichiasis.** This is a double row of eye lashes, which severely irritates the eye, causing corneal damage and, if untreated, blindness.

- **Entropian.** The eyelid (usually the lower one) turns inward, with the hairs irritating the eye.

- **Ectropian.** The eyelids droop outward, sometimes to the point of not adequately protecting the eye.

- **Persistent pupillary membrane.** This disease may cause corneal opacities or cataracts.

> **Bet You Didn't Know**
> The Canine Eye Registration Foundation (CERF) maintains a listing of dogs whose eyes have been examined by a licensed veterinary ophthalmologist. Thus, breeders can eliminate from their breeding program dogs with eye defects or dogs who have produced puppies who later developed eye defects.

Deafness

As previously noted, the gene that produces the dapple (or merle) color patterns has been associated with deafness as well as eye defects. Again, excess white markings on the head, especially around the ears, seem to "flag" this defect.

The Skin

Although most Dachsies have few skin problems, other than perhaps a reaction to fleas, there are a few skin problems found in the breed:

- **Allergies.** Dogs can be allergic to many things, including grass, pollen, dust mites, flea bites, and even the common flea collar. Some Dachsies may have food allergies as well.

- **Puppy acne (impetigo).** Small white pustules appear on the lower chin. They may open and drain much like acne in people. It usually disappears with maturity.

- **Acanthosis nigrans.** The skin thickens and darkens, usually very obviously. Secondary skin infections are also common. Sometimes the joints are affected as well.

- **Alopecia.** Sometimes hair loss is due to mange, but often it is a hormone-related condition similar to male pattern baldness.

The Skeletal System

Although Dachsies are susceptible to back problems, other skeletal problems are few. Luckily! The following three problems are among the most common:

- **Hip dysplasia.** This is a deformity of the hip joint. The dog may show lameness and may not want to move or jump. This is incurable, although sometimes surgery can make the dog more comfortable. Dogs with hip dysplasia are prone to developing arthritis later in life. Although this is well known in medium- and larger-size dogs, it is being seen more and more in smaller dogs, including Dachsies.

- **Elbow dysplasia.** This is a deformity of the elbow, much like hip dysplasia, and will show up as lameness and a lack of desire to move. This is not curable, although surgery can often make the dog more comfortable.

Bet You Didn't Know

The Orthopedic Foundation for Animals (OFA) and PennHIP maintain lists of dogs who have been x-rayed for hip and elbow dysplasia or luxated patellae. Breeders can then research the lists and eliminate from their breeding plan any dog who is or has produced dogs with questionable elbows or hips.

🏠 **Luxated Patellae.** The kneecap (patella) is not held in place properly, causing the dog to hop and skip until it moves back into place. Surgery can sometimes correct this problem. Dogs with luxated patellae are prone to developing arthritis as they age.

Dachsie Wisdom

If you think your dog is showing signs of lameness, or not wanting to move, or if you suspect your dog might have a physical problem, make an appointment with your veterinarian.

Some Other Health Concerns

Dachshunds have been known to develop a few other health problems, all of which need veterinary care:

🏠 **Cushing's disease.** This disease of the adrenal glands has many symptoms, many of which may be quite vague. Obesity and sudden aging are two of the most notable signs. Blood tests can confirm the disease.

🏠 **Diabetes.** Increased thirst and frequent urination are the most common symptoms of this disease. Although diabetes is incurable, it can be controlled.

🏠 **Hypothyroidism.** The decreased production of the thyroid gland can cause many problems. The first symptoms include lethargy, weight gain, and dry hair coat. It can be treated with daily pills.

Don't Be Afraid!

Don't let these lists of potential ills frighten you! Dachsies are, as a general rule, quite strong and healthy. This list is intended to give you a reference in case symptoms or signs appear. However, remember what I said earlier: Your veterinarian is your partner in your Dachsie's good health! When in doubt, call your vet!

The Least You Need to Know

- External parasites are more than just a nuisance; they can transmit disease and make your Dachsie's life miserable.

- Internal parasites are nasty, and some can even be transmitted to people.

- Although vaccinations can prevent many deadly diseases, the vaccinations are dependent upon your Dachsie's healthy immune system.

- Dachshunds are, on the whole, very healthy but can be affected by a few different genetic or congenital disorders.

Chapter 13

Emergency First Aid

In This Chapter

- 🏠 Becoming acquainted with emergency procedures
- 🏠 Putting together an emergency first-aid kit
- 🏠 How to restrain your dog when he's injured
- 🏠 Emergency first-aid hints and tips

As active as they are, every Dachsic will—at some point in his life—hurt himself. I consider myself a careful and diligent dog owner, but my dogs, too, have been hurt on occasion. Dax cut her paw on something sharp in the backyard. (I never found what cut her, but one pad had a slice in it.) A couple years ago, she also tore off a toenail jumping out of the van. Recently, Kes cut both front feet. Riker, my youngest, broke a hind leg when he was only three months old.

As responsible dog owners, we can try to prevent as many accidents as possible, but we must also be prepared for emergencies as much as we can. If we are prepared, we can handle those emergencies with less stress. Unfortunately, we cannot call 911 for our dogs.

Know Your Veterinarian's Emergency Procedures

When Dax cut her paw, I was already aware of my vet's emergency procedures. I knew who to call and what number. Don't wait until there's an *emergency* to find out what your vet's policies are; ask now so you know. When your dog is hurt, the last thing you want to do is wait on the phone for information. You need to do something *now!*

Dog Talk

An **emergency** is generally considered to be an injury or health threat that cannot wait for treatment until the next business day. Severe injuries, shock, bleeding, broken limbs, bloat, eye injuries, and severe allergic reactions are generally considered emergencies.

I was lucky that my vet took after-hours emergency calls, but some veterinarians don't handle after-hours emergencies at all; they refer their clients to emergency animal hospitals. Neither policy is right or wrong, as long as you understand the policy and know whom to call when that emergency happens.

If your vet refers emergencies to a local emergency animal hospital, do you know where it is? Can you find it right away without having to search for it? If you aren't sure, you should drive around and find it. Again, don't wait for the emergency before you have to look for it.

Dachsie Wisdom

You might want to consider having one credit card just for pet emergencies. That way you will never have to worry whether you have enough money to pay for an emergency vet bill.

What are your veterinarian's policies regarding payment for emergency care? What are the policies of the emergency animal hospital? Many require complete payment upon services. If that's the case, can you pay it? What happens if an emergency happens between pay days?

Post the vet's telephone number or the emergency animal hospital's number in several prominent locations. Put it on the refrigerator, in your telephone book, in your wallet, and in the first-aid kit.

A Canine First-Aid Kit

I put together my first canine first-aid kit more than 25 years ago and am always thankful I did. I've used it for a few real emergencies and numerous minor ones. I've taken care of my dogs, cats, and reptiles, as well as friends' and neighbors' dogs. It has come in handy more times than I can count.

I use a large fishing tackle box to hold all my supplies. I keep this in my van, because this is the vehicle I use to transport my dogs when we go to play, for walks, or to dog training classes. When I'm home, the van is in the driveway, so it's always available.

Some supplies you may want to keep in your first-aid kit include the following:

Large and small tweezers

Round-ended scissors and pointed sharp scissors

Disposable razors

Nail clippers (for dogs)

Thermometer

Safety pins

Mirror

Pen and pencil

Paper for notes and directions

Tape of various sizes, widths, and types

Butterfly adhesive bandages

Rolls of gauze or fabric of different widths

Gauze pads of different sizes, including eye pads

Elastic wraparound bandages (enough to wrap around your dog several times)

Instant cold compresses

Antiseptic cleansing wipes

Sterile saline eye wash

Alcohol prep pads

A small bottle of hydrogen peroxide

Benadryl tablets

Bactine

Bacitracin ointment

Kaopectate tablets or liquid

A leash and collar

Know how to use all these materials and how they work. You might even want to enroll in a Red Cross first-aid class. The Red Cross has classes for first aid for both people and pets, and attending these classes is never a bad idea. You should also know what dosages to give your dog. For example, if you are camping somewhere and your Dachsie gets stung by a bee and his nose begins to swell, how much Benadryl should you give him? Talk to your veterinarian and ask for some emergency first-aid guidance for situations such as this.

I also keep a gallon jug of water in my van, a dog bowl, and an old sheet that can be used as a stretcher.

Dachsie Wisdom

I have dog leashes in several different places, including in the car and in the first-aid kit. I don't want to have to go searching for a leash when there's an emergency; I want one to be right there when I need it.

You will need to check your first-aid kit often to replace materials that have been used and materials or medications that have expired. Most medications have an expiration date; don't use them after that date—most will become ineffective, but some even become toxic.

The Most Important Thing

The most important thing you will need during an emergency can't be put in your first-aid kit. You need a calm and clear mind. You can't get excited, and you can't panic. If you do, you won't be thinking clearly and will make mistakes or forget knowledge you already learned.

In addition, if you are excited and afraid, your dog will be, too, and might panic, hurting himself and potentially biting you or someone trying to care for him.

If you feel yourself beginning to panic, stop for a second, take a deep breath, and tell yourself, "Calm!" Then go back to what you were doing. If you have to, keep repeating the word *calm* over and over again. Make it your emergency mantra.

When the emergency is over and your dog is okay, or he's under your vet's care, you can cry your eyes out if you need to. That's okay and perfectly acceptable and normal. Just keep your calm when your dog needs you.

Know How to Restrain Your Dachsie

You must know how to restrain your Dachsie should he get hurt. This is necessary so he doesn't continue to hurt himself by struggling and so he won't hurt you when you try to help him. As much as we feel that our dogs are a part of our family, they are dogs; when a dog is hurt, he doesn't stop to think about how his struggles may hurt himself or you. And Dachsies are very strong dogs for their size!

When Kes cut both front paws, the veterinarian decided she didn't need stitches but he wanted to trim off the flaps of skin hanging from her pads. We put her on the table, and as the veterinarian's technician held her leg, I held Kes's head. He sprayed a local antiseptic and anesthetic on the cuts (which obviously stung), and as he did that, I told Kes to be still. Although the spray did sting and Kes rolled her eyes at me, she stayed still so he could take care of her cuts and bandage them. If the vet couldn't have worked on her like this, he would have had to sedate her, and there is a risk that goes along with that. But because Kes is well trained, because she trusts me, and because we have practiced restraint, the vet was able to work on her without sedating her.

Can You Muzzle Your Dachsie?

Anytime a dog is hurt enough to cry out in fear or pain, I muzzle him. I don't care if the hurt dog is one of my well-trained, trusted dogs or a neighbor's dog who has had no training at all; I muzzle the dog. A dog who is in pain will not think first; if he's hurt he may lash out in reaction to the pain and bite. By muzzling him—closing his mouth, gently but firmly—I can make sure he doesn't bite anyone when he's afraid or hurt.

You can make a muzzle out of just about anything that is long and soft. A leash works very well, as does a bandanna or a length of gauze from your first-aid kit. A leg (or two!) of panty hose also works well. Take the length of leash or material and wrap it quickly around your dog's muzzle at least two times. Wrap it gently—not too tight—but firmly. Then pull the ends back behind your dog's ears and tie it behind the neck. If you gently pull on the material around the muzzle it shouldn't slip off.

Watch Out!

Watch your dog carefully when he's muzzled. Make sure he can breathe. If he's having trouble breathing or is getting even more anxious, loosen the muzzle slightly.

Practice this muzzling technique on your Dachsie every once in a while. Make a game out of it using a happy tone of voice. Give him a treat and make a big deal out of it when you take the muzzle off. He's not going to care for it no matter what you do, but the practice will be good for you—to see how quickly you can get the muzzle on securely—and if he's felt the muzzle before, it won't be quite so traumatic when you need to do it for real.

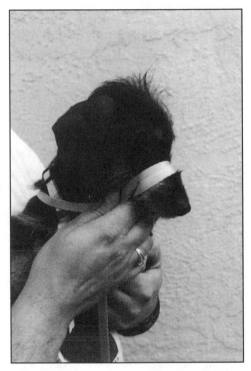

Your dog might bite if he's injured, so practice muzzling him with a leash.

Be Still!

Another skill to teach your Dachsie is to be still while lying on his side. Lay him down with his feet away from you so his head is by your right hand. Use your hand to keep his head down as you tell him, "Be still!" If he's thrashing around or trying to fight you, talk gently to him and rub his tummy. As he relaxes, tell him quietly what a good dog he is.

This is an important skill for times when you may need him to be still and quiet, especially in emergencies, so practice this every

Dachsie Wisdom
Teach your dog that "Be still!" means "Turn into a statue!"

once in a while. I practice it during our grooming sessions. While I'm brushing a back leg or combing out behind the ears, I might tell my dog, "Kes, be still!" I'll continue combing for a few seconds and then release her and praise her.

Canine CPR

CPR has saved thousands of people's lives, and it can do the same for many dogs. If you know how to perform canine CPR, you might be able to help—either your dog or someone else's treasured pet—in times of emergency.

First of all, when you see a dog lying still, you will want to make a quick evaluation prior to doing anything:

🐾 Check whether there is a heart beat.

🐾 Check whether he's breathing.

🐾 If he's not breathing, clear his mouth of any obstructions.

🐾 Pull the tongue out and to the side of his mouth so it doesn't block the airway.

🐾 Close his mouth and pull his lips over his teeth to help make his mouth airtight.

Bet You Didn't Know
In many areas, the Red Cross offers classes for pet CPR just as they do for people. Call your local Red Cross to see if they're offering a class in your area.

🐾 Inhale a deep breath, then exhale into the dog's nose. Watch his chest for it to rise after you blow.

🐾 Repeat every 10 seconds for big dogs and more often (if you can without hyperventilating yourself) for smaller dogs.

🏠 After 10 breaths, stop and do some chest compressions. Place him on his side, compress the chest five times, and go back to giving him breaths. Do 10 breaths, then 5 chest compressions, then repeat the process.

Once you start CPR, continue it until your dog starts breathing again, until you can get your dog to help, or until it seems very obvious that it is vain. But don't stop too soon; many dogs have been saved by canine CPR.

Watch Out!
Do *not* practice CPR on a dog who isn't in a life-threatening situation. You could severely hurt him, especially if he struggles (and he will!).

Practice restraining your dog so he can be cared for without hurting you or himself.

Shock Is Life Threatening!

A dog (like a person) will go into shock after a traumatic injury, in an allergic situation, or during a serious, sudden illness. By itself, shock is life-threatening, and when it's combined with what caused the shock in the first place, your dog could be in serious danger.

Symptoms of shock include the following:

- A rise in heart rate, often irregular
- Panting or very rapid breathing; often gasping
- Dilated pupils; a staring, glazed look to the eyes; and no response to movement

You can't treat your dog for shock on your own, other than keeping him warm, keeping him still, and getting him to a veterinarian right away. This isn't the time to watch the dog and hope he'll come out of it on his own; he needs help right away!

Other Threats to Your Dachsie

There are several other threats you should be aware of, both to prevent when possible, or so that you know how to respond in an emergency.

Heatstroke

Many Dachsies are so tenacious and stubborn that they will continue their activities—playful or serious—until they are physically exhausted and in danger of heatstroke. Because your Dachsie may not stop when he needs to, it's up to you to make sure you keep your dog safe—especially in warm weather.

Dogs don't sweat through pores in the skin as people do. Instead, dogs lose heat by panting and by sweating through the pads of their feet. Because of this, dogs can overheat much more quickly than

people do. A dog who is overheating will lay down, often by flopping himself down, or will pace back and forth in agitation. He will be panting heavily and may go into shock. His body temperature will rise rapidly. You will need to cool him down immediately. Immerse him in cool water or pack him in ice and get him to the vet's office *now!*

Watch Out!
Dogs left in parked cars are at extreme risk of dying from heat stroke. The inside of a parked car can heat up to over 100 degrees even when the outside temperature may only be in the 70s.

Bleeding

Bleeding—either internal or external—occurs after just about any injury. How it should be treated depends on the type of bleeding and its severity.

If the skin isn't broken, there may be bleeding under the skin. This can result in a bruise if the injury is small. A bruise can be treated by applying an ice pack wrapped in a wash cloth at 15-minute intervals until it seems that the bleeding under the skin has stopped. After 24 hours, use a heat pack to improve circulation to the area to promote healing.

Bleeding from small scrapes, scratches, and small cuts is usually not a danger to your Dachsie. Simply wipe the blood off, apply pressure with a gauze pad if it's still oozing, and when the bleeding stops, rinse the injured area with hydrogen peroxide or nolvalsan. Check it regularly for a few days to make sure the injury isn't infected and that it's healing okay.

Bet You Didn't Know
A bag of frozen vegetables such as corn or peas makes an excellent ice pack.

If the wound is red and oozing, rinse it several times a day with hydrogen peroxide and carefully rub an antibiotic ointment on it. If you're concerned, make an appointment to bring your dog in to see the vet. This is not, however, an emergency.

A continuous oozing type of bleeding is more serious. You will need to put pressure on the wound, using layers of gauze pads and pressure from your hand, and you'll want to get the dog to your veterinarian right away. Stitches will probably be required, and if the dog has lost a lot of blood, additional treatments may be needed.

Bleeding that comes out in spurts is very dangerous; it means that a major blood vessel has been broken and your dog is in immediate danger of bleeding to death. Use a length of gauze or a shoelace to make a tourniquet above the wound, between the wound and the heart. Wrap the shoelace around the dog's leg, then tie a small stick to the knot. Twist the stick so that it tightens the knot and the shoelace around the leg. You are trying to cut off circulation so that the bleeding slows.

> **Watch Out!**
> Watch your dog carefully. A significant blood loss can trigger shock and cardiac arrest. Get him to the vet's office right away!

> **Watch Out!**
> A tourniquet can cause as much damage as a serious wound, so use it only when the dog is in danger of bleeding to death. For all other wounds, use hand pressure on the wound to slow the bleeding.

Tourniquets *must* be loosened every 10 to 15 minutes, or the leg will die due to lack of circulation. Loosen it, let the blood flow for a couple minutes, then tighten it again. Many specialists recommend not using a tourniquet because most people don't know how to use them correctly.

Internal Injuries

If you believe your Dachsie may have internal injuries, keep him still. If he has been hit by a car or bicycle, kicked, run over by a larger dog, or has had other hard trauma to the body, have him lie still and keep him still. If his crate is nearby, put him in it. If you have to, you can restrain him on a board. Suspected internal injuries should be seen by the vet as soon as possible.

Seizures

If your Dachsie has a seizure, try to keep him safe, but don't try to restrain him. Most seizures last only a minute or two (although they seem like forever). If this is a first seizure, get your dog to the vet's office within 24 hours of the seizure, as blood tests can often show why the dog had the seizure.

If your dog has a seizure disorder, your vet can guide you as to how to manage it and how to handle your dog during seizures.

Dachsie Wisdom

My dog Dax had a mild seizure when her liver was inflamed. The blood test showed the liver problem, we medicated her and got the liver healthy again, and she has not had any other seizures since.

Choking

Dachsies who like to play catch with balls risk choking on their favorite toy. Make sure the ball you throw for your dog is large enough that your dog cannot choke on it. Even a tennis ball may be too small for some standard Dachsies. If your Dachsie catches the ball in the back of his mouth (instead of with his teeth), teach him to play Frisbee instead!

Dogs—especially puppies—put stuff in their mouth all the time; after all, they don't have hands, and tasting and chewing on stuff is one of the ways puppies discover their world. Unfortunately, these dogs are in danger from choking on things.

If your dog is gasping, choking, gagging, or has stopped breathing, try the following:

- ⌂ Open his mouth and see if you can see what is blocking his airway.

- ⌂ If you can reach whatever is blocking the airway, do so and pull it out. Sometimes tongs (like salad tongs) or needled-nose pliers will help you grasp round things, such as a ball.

- ⌂ If you can't grasp the object, try the canine version of the Heimlich maneuver. Stand above and behind your dog, reach under his belly just behind the rib cage, and pull up quickly several times.

- ⌂ If this doesn't work, don't waste time, his life is at stake—get him to the nearest veterinarian right away.

Poisons

Hopefully, you dog-proofed your house, yard, and garage before you brought your Dachsie home, and all dangers were removed from his reach. Unfortunately, accidents can still happen, and more than one Dachsie has been poisoned because he was too curious and stuck his nose where it didn't belong.

Symptoms of poisoning can vary depending on what caused it. Some of the more common symptoms include extreme salivation and drooling, vomiting, diarrhea, and muscle tremors. The Dachsie's eyes may be dilated, or he may suffer seizures.

If your Dachsie ingests any poisonous substance, it's always a good idea to call your vet right away so you know what to do. Following are some of the more common substances found around the house and some steps you can take if your Dachsie gets into them:

- ⌂ **Antifreeze.** Induce vomiting and get your Dachsie to the vet's office right away.

🐾 **Bleach.** Induce vomiting and take your Dachsie to your veterinarian soon, although if he's vomited right away, it's no longer an emergency.

Bet You Didn't Know
You can get your Dachsie to vomit by giving him several teaspoons of hydrogen peroxide.

🐾 **Chocolate.** This is poisonous to dogs, so make him vomit and then call your vet.

🐾 **Gasoline.** Give him some vegetable oil to block absorption, and take him to the vet's office right away.

🐾 **Ibuprofen.** Make him vomit, and get him to the vet's office right away.

🐾 **Insecticides.** If ingested, get him to the vet right away. Do not induce vomiting unless your vet recommends it. If there was skin contact, wash him thoroughly, then get him to the vet's right away.

🐾 **Rat, mouse, roach, or snail poisons.** Induce vomiting, and get him to your vet's office right away.

Bring whatever it was your Dachsie got into with you to your vet's office. If at all possible, bring the label with the name of the product and any ingredients. The more information you can give your vet, the better.

Dachsie Wisdom
The National Poison Control Center maintains a 24-hour poison hotline: 1-900-680-0000. No credit card is needed; your phone bill will be charged.

Gastric Torsion or Bloat

Gastric torsion, also called bloat, is more prevalent in large breed dogs with a deep chest, such as Great Danes, Rottweilers, German Shepherds, and Labrador Retrievers. However, it can happen to just

about any breed, including our deep-chested Dachsies. When a dog bloats, stomach gases cause the abdomen to distend. If too much pressure occurs, the stomach can actually twist (torsion). Shock follows quickly, and the dog dies.

 **Bet You Didn't Know**
Sometimes bloat happens for no known reason; however, you can lessen the chances of it happening by keeping the dog quiet for an hour after each meal, feeding two small meals instead of one large meal, and limiting water for an hour after each meal.

If you notice your dog pacing, showing extreme restlessness, and gagging (without throwing up), and he has a distended abdomen, especially soon after eating, get him to the vet's office right away. Bloat can be often be treated successfully if you get your dog to the vet's office soon enough.

Burns

Burns can happen in a variety of ways. Thermal burns are those caused by heat, and curious Dachsies can be burned if they investigate a candle or knock over the iron. Electrical burns occur when a Dachsie chews on an electrical cord, chews on a battery, or licks an electrical outlet. Chemical burns happen when the Dachsie makes contact with a corrosive substance that causes a burn. These could include bleach, gasoline, liquid drain cleaners, paint thinners, or road salt.

If you suspect your Dachsie has been burned, follow these directions:

- If the burn is chemical in nature, rinse your Dachsie thoroughly. Treat it also as a potential poisoning.

- For any burn, put an ice pack on the spot.

- If the burn is not severe and the skin is simply red, keep it clean and watch it carefully to make sure it doesn't get infected.

- If the burn has damaged layers of skin; is blistered, bleeding, and oozing; or has damaged all of the layers of skin, take your Dachsie to the vet's office right away.

Insect Bites and Stings

Any Dachsie who spends any amount of time outside will someday run up against a bug that doesn't want to play with him. Most insect bites and stings are simply an annoyance and no real health threat; however, some dogs are allergic to bee stings or wasp stings. In addition, some spider bites or scorpion stings can be quite dangerous.

If you suspect your dog has been stung or bitten by an insect, first try to find where on your dog's body the bite or sting happened. If there is a stinger, scrape it out. Don't grab it and pull it; that will squeeze more venom into your dog's skin. Scrape it out with a fingernail. If you need to, shave away some of the dog's hair so you can see the sting or bite. Wash it off, pour some hydrogen peroxide on it, and watch it.

While watching for a reaction, try to identify the insect. If it is a scorpion, a black widow spider, a recluse spider, or another poisonous insect, call your veterinarian right away—don't wait for signs of an allergic reaction.

If you can't find the insect or cannot identify it, watch for an allergic reaction. Some signs of allergic reaction include the following:

- Swelling at the site of the bite or sting and in the body tissues surrounding it

- Redness or extreme whiteness

- Fever

- Muscle ache, joint pain, and lameness

- Breathing difficulty

- Vomiting or diarrhea

 **Dachsie Wisdom**

I keep a supply of Benadryl in my first-aid kit at all times because two of my dogs are allergic to bees.

If your Dachsie is showing any of these allergic reactions, call your veterinarian right away. He may recommend that you give your Dachsie a Benadryl antihistamine immediately to combat some of the allergic reaction. He will also want to see your Dachsie as soon as you can bring him in.

Animal Bites

If your Dachsie is bitten by another dog during play time and the bite is a simple puncture with teeth, don't be too worried. Simply wash the bite, pour some hydrogen peroxide over the bite, and watch it. If it looks red and possibly infected, call your veterinarian.

However, if your Dachsie is attacked by an unknown dog, call your vet immediately, as this could pose a serious health threat. If you can, try to find the dog's owner to make sure the dog is vaccinated, especially with an up-to-date rabies vaccine.

If your dog is bitten by an unknown cat or a wild animal, you must get him to the veterinarian's office right away. If your Dachsie has received his rabies vaccination (usually given between four and six months of age and updated regularly) that worry will be eliminated. However, if your Dachsie is a puppy and has not yet received that vaccine, there could be serious consequences. Your vet will also want to treat the wound itself and might recommend antibiotics.

> **Watch Out!**
> Skunks, raccoons, bats, and squirrels have all been known to be infected with rabies. The best prevention is to make sure your Dachsie is vaccinated.

Snake Bites

Contrary to their reputation, most snakes are nonaggressive. In fact, most of the time you won't see the snakes that are close to you; they will slither away before you know they are near. However, many snakes will defend themselves when threatened; and when your Dachsie decides to use a snake as a play toy, the snake will consider that a threat! Luckily, the vast majority of snakes are nonvenomous (not poisonous).

If your dog is bitten by a nonvenomous snake, just wash the wound with hydrogen peroxide and watch it to make sure the wound doesn't get infected.

If your dog is bitten by a venomous snake, don't panic. First of all, many snakes don't automatically inject venom. Snakes use venom to subdue prey, and your dog is not a natural dinner item for snakes (fortunately!). Therefore, the snake may strike to scare away your dog without actually injecting venom.

If venom is injected, your dog will begin to swell. If he was bitten on the leg, the leg will swell. Unfortunately, most dogs are bitten on the face because they stick their nose down into the snake's space and whap!—the snake strikes the dog on the nose or muzzle. If the nose or muzzle begins to swell, the dog is in great danger of suffocating, so get him to the veterinarian's office right away. Call ahead so the vet can make arrangements to get the antivenin.

Before leaving for the vet's office, take a good, hard look at the snake—without getting bit yourself, of course! Make sure you can describe it or identify it in a book. There is no universal antivenin for all snakes; each species has its own antivenin, and you need to be able to identify the particular species. Look in particular at the shape of the head—is it triangular in shape or elongated? What are the color patterns on the snake? Is there a diamond-shaped color pattern, or does the snake have bands of color around the body? All these things can help you and your vet identify the snake in question.

Natural (and Other) Disasters

Where do you live? In Southern California, we must deal with wildfires and earthquakes. In the Midwest, dog owners must put up with tornadoes. The Northeast has blizzards. Residents of Florida must be able to survive hurricanes. Natural disasters are a fact of life, and you need to make preparations so you can take care of your Dachsie as well as your family.

In my garage, within reach of the side door, is my emergency kit in case of earthquakes or fires. I use a plastic trash can with a tight-fitting lid. In it are my emergency supplies. It has some canned dog food that will keep a long time, a can opener, water, a smaller first-aid kit, and a variety of other supplies that are recommended for people, including some blankets, towels, and soap.

A few of my neighbors think I'm either a little neurotic or overly concerned to have made these preparations. However, my husband and I have lived in this area for many years and have been evacuated due to wildfires twice. When ordered to evacuate, you don't have any time to put stuff together. You grab what you can and leave. My emergency kit has come in handy for both of those situations, and it's there for any future emergencies.

An emergency kit isn't difficult to put together and does not have to be expensive. However, if you ever need it, it is worth all the effort. As one who has had to use that kit, I can tell you from experience I am very happy I put one together!

The Least You Need to Know

- Before an emergency occurs, know what your veterinarian's emergency procedures are, including his payment policies.

- Know how to restrain your Dachsie so he can be handled in an emergency.

- Put together a first-aid kit, keep it stocked and handy, and know the emergency phone numbers for your vet and poison control center.

- Know what to do in an emergency.

Part  4

Dachshund Decorum

All Dachsies have their own opinion as to how they should behave. Unfortunately, that opinion isn't always the best one for Dachsie owners! So in the following chapters, you'll learn how to teach your Dachsie and how to motivate him so that he wants to be good.

You'll learn how to teach the basic commands Sit, Down, Stay, Come, and Heel. You'll also learn how to prevent, handle, and solve behavior problems such as digging, barking, and jumping on people. If you're wondering why your Dachsie does some things—such as sniff other dogs' feces or get into the cat's litter box—you'll find the answers here.

Although dogs have been our companions for thousands of years, they don't automatically know how to behave properly or obey commands; each individual dog must be taught what behavior is appreciated and what isn't. The same goes for dog owners—it takes time and training to understand why dogs do what they do and how to get them to do what *you* want them to do.

Some Dachsie owners say their breed is untrainable, but don't you believe it!

14

Teaching You to Train Your Dachshund

In This Chapter

- 🏠 How to train your Dachsie
- 🏠 A variety of training techniques and tools
- 🏠 Being your Dachsie's leader
- 🏠 Tips to make your training more successful

Recently, I was talking to several Dachshund owners who were interested in therapy dog training. I told them about our therapy dog group and encouraged them to participate. However, when I told them that obedience training was necessary for potential therapy dogs, I was told, "Dachsies don't do well in obedience training!"

As a dog trainer, I am always amazed when people tell me Dachshunds are untrainable. I will agree that Dachshunds are tough little dogs and that they can be quite independent and stubborn, but those characteristics don't mean the breed is untrainable! Dachshunds are intelligent dogs, and many have learned to train their owners quite well—including convincing their owners that dog training is a waste of time!

How sad! Without training, there is so much you and your dog can't do. In addition, your relationship suffers. There's nothing quite like the bond between a dog and owner who understand each other, communicate well with each other, and cooperate with each other. And that's what good dog training is!

Understanding Dog Training

When you train your Dachsie, you aren't trying to turn him into a robot. Instead, you are trying to communicate with him and motivate him so that he wants to cooperate with you. When you and your dog both want to accomplish the same goals, training is easy.

Take a moment to consider your goals for training your Dachsie. Are you interested in therapy dog volunteer work? Do you want your Dachsie to be a well-behaved family pet? Would you like to compete in obedience trials? Most dog owners today want a well-behaved family pet, but many people also want to participate in dog activities or sports. Basic obedience training is necessary for all Dachsies, but after basic training, you should have an idea of where you would like this training to go. What are your goals for you and your Dachsie?

Dachsie Wisdom _____
When thinking about future goals, don't sell your Dachsie short. Many Dachsie owners participate in dog sports quite successfully. In 2001, more than 125 agility titles were earned by Dachsies, as well as 599 conformation championships, about 100 obedience titles, two dozen tracking titles, more than 60 field championships, and almost 100 earth dog titles.

Instead of following the crowd or falling for the myth that Dachshunds cannot be trained, visualize your Dachsie accomplishing your training goals. Your Dachshund *can* be trained, and the two of you *can* have fun while doing so.

Books, Videos, Classes, Private Training: Which One?

Chapter 15 gives you a good description of how to teach your Dachsie the basic commands. In addition, I'll discuss a number of the most commonly seen behavior problems. Is that going to be enough? For some dogs, yes, this will be perfectly adequate. For others, no, it may not be. I'm not trying to weasel out of anything by giving you a seemingly wishy-washy answer, but it's true!

Dachsies who are basically good dogs might need only rudimentary basic obedience training. If their owners are good at following directions and simply want their dog to be a good family pet, then this book may be all that's needed.

Other dogs (or owners!) may need more. Group classes provide a lot of socialization to other dogs and considerable distractions. Some dogs need this stimulation; others need to learn to ignore the disruptions. Group classes are particularly good for puppies who need socialization.

Private training is quieter and allows the instructor to work one on one with the dog and owner. Some owners need this special attention, especially many first-time dog owners.

Videos put words into pictures. For dog owners who are very visual, sometimes these can be good sources of additional information.

You need to find what is going to work best for you. Maybe it will be a combination of things—this book, a group class, and maybe a private lesson or two to help you over the rough spots. It's up to you. The nice thing is that these alternatives are available!

Watch Out!
If your Dachsie growls menacingly at you, snarls (shows teeth), snaps or bites, call a trainer for help immediately!

Treats can be a great training tool in motivating your Dachsie to cooperate with training.

Training Methods

Every dog trainer, dog obedience instructor, or canine behaviorist (as well as this dog book author!) has his or her own favorite method or technique for training dogs or changing dog behavior. Why?

Dachsie Wisdom

Make sure you're comfortable with any training method you use. If you aren't comfortable, ask questions or look around for another trainer. The decision how to train your Dachsie rests with you.

Well, first of all, dog behavior is a very inexact science. Every single dog—even every Dachsie—is going to respond to training in a different way. When you combine this with the fact that every dog owner adds his or her own variations, you can see why it isn't an exact science at all.

The best training methods take into consideration that every dog and every dog owner are unique individuals. Allowances should be made for different responses, and alternative techniques should be available.

Balanced Training

Quite a few dog trainers today advocate training methods that use only *positive reinforcements*. These techniques reward the dog for good behavior but do not correct the dog when he makes a mistake. Although in theory this type of training sounds wonderful, it's not the right training technique for many dogs, including most Dachshunds.

> **Dog Talk**
> A **positive reinforcement** is something the dog likes, such as food treats, a toy, petting, and verbal praise.

Keep training as positive as possible, but remember that corrections are often needed.

With training techniques using only positive reinforcement, the dog is supposed to work for the positive reinforcements, and when one isn't given, understand *why* it isn't given. For example, when teaching your dog to sit, the dog is rewarded for sitting but is ignored when he doesn't sit. Ideally, the dog will realize he's being ignored and will then sit for the reward.

Can you see your Dachsie doing that? Unfortunately, most Dachsies are entirely too busy and too curious and find the world so self-rewarding that ignoring their bad behavior in the hopes that it might stop just doesn't work.

Instead, Dachshunds do better with a training technique that balances positive reinforcements with *corrections* that let the dog know when he's made a mistake. This balance makes things very clear to the dog. He learns when he's doing something right and when he's making a mistake. There is no confusion and no guessing on his part.

Dog Talk

A **correction** is something that gets the dog's attention as he's making a mistake, such as saying "No!" or snapping and releasing the leash.

Training Tools

Training tools are things you use to help train your Dachsie. A leash is a training tool, as are collars. Your voice is a training tool, too. Anything you use during training can be considered a training tool.

The Leash

Leashes aren't only used for taking dogs on walks. The leash can also be used to help teach your Dachsie to respond to your verbal commands. For example, if your Dachsie is galloping down the hall with one of your slippers in his mouth, you can call to him and ask him to drop the slipper. If he ignores you and continues playing keep away, he has just learned that you cannot enforce your commands. However, if he has the leash on as he dashes past, you can stop him, take the slipper away, then walk him over to one of his toys and show him what he can play with.

You can attach the leash to your dog's collar anytime he is close to you and you can actively supervise him. Always take it off when you can't watch him so he doesn't get it tangled and choke himself.

Watch Out!
Never leave the leash on your dog when you cannot supervise him.

Training Collars

You'll be amazed at the variety of training collars available at pet-supply stores. Most trainers begin puppies on a flat nylon or leather buckle-type collar. This is a soft collar that doesn't give hard corrections. As the Dachsie gets older, most trainers switch the dog to a chain collar, often called a choke chain. This collar works with a snap and release correction (like a bouncing ball—snap and release) and should never be allowed to tighten and remain tight on the dog's neck because it can potentially choke the dog. The chain collar should never remain on the dog when you can't supervise him.

Another good training tool that's similar to a collar is a head halter. These work much like the halter on a horse and are used to guide the dog's head. Head halters are good for Dachsies who pull hard and choke themselves on a regular collar. The downfall is that many Dachsies really don't like the head halters. However, they can get used to them, and if a trainer suggests that a head halter might be the best training tool for your Dachsie, go ahead and try it.

Motivators

You'll also want something to help motivate your dog during training. Your voice is a good motivator. A happy, "Ice cream!" tone of voice can tell your Dachsie, "Good boy!" Other motivators might be food treats, a tennis ball, or a squeaky toy. A motivator only works when your Dachsie likes it, so find something that makes your dog excited and then use that as a training tool.

Your Voice

Your voice is your most important training tool. My ultimate goal is to teach my dogs to listen to my voice, pay attention, and respond to verbal commands when off the leash. For example, if one of my dogs is playing out in a field, sniffing and chasing rabbits, I want to be able to call her back to me and I want her to listen to that command and respond to it right away with no hesitation. I also want her to listen to me around the house, in the car, and in the backyard. I want her to understand that I don't just jabber on for no reason, and that she should pay attention to me when I talk to her.

To make it easier for the dog to understand, you will be copying some of the mother dog's verbalizations—or at least her tone of voice. When your Dachsie was still with his mom, he would interact with her and his littermates using verbal sounds as well as body language. If he wanted to play, his bark was higher in pitch. If a littermate or his mom responded to his play invitation, their barks were also higher in pitch.

We can make a safe assumption that play invitations are higher in pitch than the normal speaking voice, and we can use that to our advantage. When praising your Dachsie, say "Good boy!" in the tone of voice you used to say "Ice cream!" as a child. This should be higher in tone from your normal speaking voice but not as high pitched as a yelp that would mean hurt.

Watch Out!

Don't correct your Dachsie with a deep voice and then giggle; you will lose all authority!

When your Dachsie was corrected by his mom—for example, if he bit her with his needle-sharp baby teeth—she would growl at him. That deep growl meant, "You made a mistake! Don't do it again."

We can use this sound, too, to our advantage. When your Dachsie makes a mistake, you can use a deep voice to make a sound such as "Acckk!"

Of course, there is no way we can sound exactly like a dog—even with lots of practice. What you are trying to do is use your voice in the same way your Dachsie's mom used hers—higher pitched for happy, very high pitched for hurt, and deeper sounding for correction. By using tones much like she used, you are hoping to keep confusion during training to a minimum.

If you are normally soft spoken and are concerned about using your voice to control your Dachsie, don't worry. Use your normal speaking volume (loudness) but vary the tones just as someone else who speaks more loudly would do. You are teaching your Dachsie to listen to you, and if you are naturally soft spoken, that's fine. Your Dachsie can hear you very well.

Dachsie Wisdom

Do not scream or holler at your dog; he can hear very well. Speak in normal tones. When correcting your Dachsie, use the "Acckk!" in a firm tone, sounding like you mean what you say, but do not yell.

Putting It Together

You will teach your Dachsie by helping him do what it is you want him to do, by praising and rewarding him when he does it, and by letting him know when he makes a mistake. Praise alone will not teach him, nor will corrections alone.

For example, if your Dachsie is jumping up on you, you can tell him, "Acckk! No jump!" as he leaps up on you. That alone is not enough to stop the problem, though. If you follow that by shaping him into a Sit and telling him, "Good boy to sit!" and pet him while he's sitting, he learns an acceptable alternative.

Bet You Didn't Know
When your dog is doing something right *always* praise him. Don't worry if you hadn't told him to do it this time. Praise him anyway! If he sits on his own when you get out his leash to go for a walk, for example, praise him for sitting!

Let's look at it this way:

- He's jumping on you for attention.

- Correct the jumping when he leaps at you.

- Show him a better way: Have him sit in front of you.

- Praise and pet him for sitting.

Much of your Dachsie's training can be approached in this manner. Let him know when he's made a mistake, but also show him what he can do instead. Show him the right way and praise him enthusiastically for doing the right thing.

The Agony of Negative Attention

Some dogs, just like some children, will actually work for negative attention (corrections). These confused souls have discovered that they get attention when they misbehave and are willing to put up with the yelling, collar corrections, and other negative attention because, after all, it is attention. For these dogs, attention is anything that you do to him, whether it's negative or positive.

Often, these dogs have some problem behaviors and are frequently in trouble. Their owners usually yell at them more than anything else, so the dog soon equates yelling with owner attention. So he continues to get into trouble just so he can get attention, any attention, even negative attention.

To change this scenario, the owner must focus on giving the dog attention for good behavior. This might be difficult in the beginning because you will need to give less attention to the bad behavior. However, when the negative attention decreases and the good behavior is rewarded, the dog's focus will change.

This will take a restructuring of how you react to your dog, though, and it may be very difficult in the beginning. However, you will find that as you decrease corrections and emphasize the positives, your attitude toward your dog will change. You will find yourself liking him more, and that will give you more motivation to continue.

You Must Be Your Dachsie's Leader

Most Dachshunds are tenacious and pushy, many can be stubborn and hard headed, and quite a few are very dominant. That's not to say this is bad; that's what they were bred to be. A wimpy dog couldn't hunt badgers! However, in the family and in relationships with people, a tenacious, stubborn, dominant dog can sometimes—no, let's be honest, can often—be a problem.

Therefore, it's very important that you establish yourself as your Dachsie's leader. You are not your Dachsie's best friend—at least not yet—nor should you try to be. Instead, be your Dachsie's leader. If he were living with other dogs instead of people, an older dog would assume the leadership position. This dog would demand certain behaviors or actions from subordinates, of which your Dachsie would be one.

In my family right now, Dax is my oldest dog at seven years of age. She is the leader (of the dogs), although she does recognize my husband's and my leadership. Kes, at five years of age, is subordinate to Dax, and shows it by giving way to Dax, by letting Dax take her toys, and by lowering herself if Dax growls at her. Riker, at three and the only boy, gives in to both of the older girls. They are very tolerant of him right now, although they do correct him when he's too obnoxious.

Now, naturally, you are not a dog, and your dog is not living in a dog pack; however, certain things still apply:

🏠 The leader is confident. If you are not yet confident about training, at least act like you are!

🏠 You should always eat first, even if it's just an apple. The leader of the pack always eats first and best.

🏠 The leader always goes first. Don't let your Dachsie dash through doorways ahead of you. Don't allow him to run out of the house or into the house ahead of you. Make him wait at all doorways, car doors, and the gate.

🏠 The leader establishes the rules. It's your house, you pay the bills, and you have every right to set some rules.

> **Dachsie Wisdom**
>
> If you don't assume the leadership role, your Dachsie will assume it as he grows up. If he assumes the job, you're in big trouble. Dogs in charge of people are usually very aggressive, dominating, and often very confused. Behavior problems abound! You *must* assume the leadership position!

The leader, according to your Dachsie, is the biggest, strongest, fastest, and smartest. Now, not all leaders actually are those things, but even if they aren't, they still act like they are. Many small dogs are the leaders of much bigger dogs; what they lack in actual size they make up for in attitude! So act like the leader!

Make Your Training Successful

You can make your training more successful by following a few guidelines:

🏠 Show your Dachsie what to do, help him do it, and praise him when he does it correctly. Use a happy tone of voice to praise and use other motivators you know your dog likes. Treats and toys are fine.

🏠 Give only one command. Do not repeat the word over and over again. If you repeat it, which time counts? Which one should he respond to? Think about what should happen if he dashes out the front door and is heading toward the street. You need to call him back to you before he gets hit by a car. If you have taught him that you will give multiple commands, he will wait for multiple commands for the Come command also. So say it once and help him do it. If he ignores you, let him know he's made a mistake.

🏠 Consistency is important. Once you establish some rules—such as keeping the Dachsie off the furniture (if that is what you want)—you and everyone in your household must consistently enforce them.

🏠 Timing is critical to your training success. Praise your Dachsie *as* he is doing something right. Correct your Dachsie *as* he makes a mistake. Praise and corrections that happen later are not effective.

🏠 Corrections—any corrections, including voice, collar, or any other training tools—should be forceful enough to stop unwanted behavior and *that's all*. Excessive corrections or after-the-fact punishment will not teach the dog effectively and could easily cause your Dachsie to shy away from you or avoid you.

Some additional training tips include the following:

🏠 You don't need to yell or scream or shout at your Dachsie. A loud, frightening voice will not stop unwanted behavior and will threaten your relationship with your dog.

🏠 You do have to mean what you say. If you correct the dog and giggle, or laugh when he makes a mistake, your Dachsie will not take you seriously. Believe in what you are doing.

🏠 Keep in mind that bad behavior is *not* directed at you personally. Your Dachsie is *not* chewing on the sofa and thinking, "Ha! I'll chew up this and that will teach him to go off to work and leave me alone!"

Watch Out! Don't train your Dachsie when the pressures of the day will cause you to take out your frustrations on him.

🐾 Don't train your Dachsie when you're angry. Never train your dog when you are drunk, stoned, tipsy, or buzzed.

Stop on a High Note

Whenever you're training your Dachsie, finish each training session by doing something your dog can do and do well. By stopping the session on a high note, you and your dog both leave with a sense of accomplishment.

This is particularly important if you or your Dachsie are having trouble. For example, if you are trying to teach your Dachsie to lie down and stay and your dog isn't cooperating, you don't want to stop the training session with both of you frustrated. So instead, have him sit and shake hands, or do a nice Sit and Stay command. Then praise him enthusiastically and quit for the time being. (Various training commands are discussed in Chapter 15.)

Later, when you have calmed down and relaxed, you can go back and work on the Lie down command some more.

The Least You Need to Know

🐾 Decide your goals for training your Dachsie. Do you want a well-behaved family pet? Do you want to participate in dog sports? A Dachsie can do it all!

🐾 Your voice, the leash and collar, and the things you use to motivate your dog are your training tools. Use them all the time, not just when you're on walks.

🐾 You must be your Dachsie's leader. It's natural, and he expects it.

🐾 Always finish your training sessions with something your Dachsie can do well and then reward him for a job well done.

Chapter 15

Teaching and Using Obedience Exercises

In This Chapter

🏠 The importance of commands

🏠 Teaching your Dachsie the eight basic commands

🏠 Using the commands at home and out in public

🏠 Tips for successful training

Come. Sit. Release. Lie down. Stay. Watch me. Let's go. Heel.

These eight basic obedience commands should be the foundation of every dog's—including every Dachshund's—training. When he knows these commands, you can build on them and do just about anything else you want to do with your Dachsie.

In addition, as you will see as you learn these commands, they can also help you stop or control many problem behaviors. For example, when your Dachsie sits to greet people, he won't be jumping up on them! Ah ha! Magic!

So start training your Dachsie today, beginning with these commands. Follow the directions for teaching, keep the training as positive as possible, and have fun while you do it!

Start with the Basics

The eight basic commands teach your Dachsie several skills, all of which are important for good behavior at home with you and out in public. Some of these commands teach your dog to control himself and to be aware that there are consequences to his actions. This is a hard exercise for many Dachsies, especially many mini Dachsies. Many mini Dachsies have never learned to hold still. Because they are small and very cute—especially as puppies—they are often allowed to bounce around with no restrictions. Unfortunately, this does the dog no good and makes it much more difficult for the dog to learn to hold still as he grows up. Ideally, Dachsie puppies should learn the concept of self-control early.

When you teach your Dachsie the concept of self-control, he will learn that if he controls himself, does what you ask of him, and restrains his desires to run and jump and play (at least for the moment), he will be praised. If he doesn't restrain himself, there will be no praise and there might be a correction.

In other situations, the command may serve as an alternative behavior to prevent problems. For example, your dog won't jump on people if he learns to sit for praise and petting. He can't pull your arm out of the socket, dragging you down the street, if he learns to walk nicely on the leash while watching you.

Any training you decide to do later with your Dachsie rests on these basic commands. He'll need to understand these thoroughly before he can go on to any advanced training or any dog activities or sports.

Teaching Sit

Kneel or sit on the floor or ground with your Dachsie. Or if you have physical limitations, lift your Dachsie up on the sofa, a bench, or a table. You just want to be close to him at this point in *Sit* training.

With your Dachsie on his leash close to you, show him a treat. When he reaches up to sniff the treat, move it over his head toward his tail as you tell him, "Sweetie-pie, Sit." When his head comes up and back to follow the treat, his hips will go down. After he sits, praise him and give him the treat.

_____ **Dog Talk** _____

Teach your Dachsie that *Sit* means he should lower his hips to the ground while his shoulders remain upright, and he should hold still until you release him.

Use a treat to shape the Dachsie into a Sit, then give the treat as a reward.

If he spins around to try and get the treat rather than sitting, put the treat away in your pocket. Put one hand on his chest where his chest and neck meet. Tell him "Sweetie-pie, Sit," and at the same time, push that hand slightly up and back (thereby pushing his chest up and back) as the other hand slides down his back toward his hips and tucks his hips down and under. Think of a teeter-totter; up and back at the chest and down and under at the hips. When he's sitting, praise him.

With both methods, when he does sit, praise him with a higher than normal tone of voice, "Good boy to Sit!" When he begins to move from position (not after he's already moved but when he begins to move), use your growling tone of voice, "Acckk!" and put him back in the Sit position.

The Sit Is Self-Control!

The Sit is a very useful command, not just as the foundation command for more advanced commands, but also for use around the house.

- 🏠 Have the dog sit to greet people, especially if he likes to jump on people. He can't jump on people and sit at the same time. Even a mini Dachsie, with those raking little claws, can be quite annoying jumping up on people.

- 🏠 Have him sit when you fix his dinner. Self-control!

- 🏠 Have him sit when you hook up his leash to take him outside. If he's sitting, he can't be spinning around in circles out of excitement.

- 🏠 Have him sit in front of the door to go inside or outside so he isn't charging through doorways.

Dachsie Wisdom

Although Dachsies—even standards—are not large dogs, they can still ruin clothes or scratch skin if they jump on people. Teaching the Sit can prevent those problems.

Have your Dachsie sit for everything. Have him sit for petting, for his dinner, for treats, and for toys. When he comes up to you and nudges you to pet him; have him sit first. When he drops his tennis ball at your feet; have him sit first.

By teaching him to sit for everything he wants, you are setting up some rules for behavior and giving him structure—which is important to a young dog—and you are giving him a job to do. Keep in mind that most of the breeds of dogs in existence today were bred to do a job of some kind. We know Dachsies were hunters, but how many of them actually hunt anymore? Other than the occasional trespasser in your yard, not many! Sitting for everything he wants can be your Dachsie's first job!

Training Close to Your Dachsie

As you begin training your Dachsie, you can make it easier for both you and your dog by kneeling or sitting on the floor close to him or by lifting him up onto the sofa or a bench. Although one of your ultimate training goals will be to talk to him and have him listen to you as you go about your daily routine (standing upright), in the beginning it's easier if you and your dog are closer together.

By being closer to him (in height) you can help him by using your hands, and you can react faster to both reward or correct him. Because timing is so important to training, being able to react quickly is vital to your success.

As both you and your Dachsie get better at the training skills, you can begin working him on the floor while you stand up. But in the beginning, don't be afraid to make it easier for both of you.

Teaching Release

Your Dachsie needs a beginning and an end to each exercise. The beginning is when you give him a command, such as "Sweetie-pie, Sit!" You will then teach him that the exercise is over when you give him a *Release* command.

When your dog is sitting, pat him on the shoulder as you tell him, "Okay!" in a happy,

___ **Dog Talk** ___
The **Release** command means, "Okay, you're done now, you can move."

high-pitched tone of voice and encourage him to get up from the Sit by raising your hands high. If you lift your hands up and bounce a little yourself, he will probably bounce up, too, copying your movements.

If he doesn't move with this hand and body motion, pat him on the shoulder as you tell him, "Okay!" in a high-pitched tone of voice and then use the leash to gently move him from the Sit.

Bet You Didn't Know
Use both a touch and a verbal command for the Release. If you use only a word, the dog could release himself whenever he hears that word used in conversation!

The primary purpose of the Release command is to let the dog know when he's free to move from a previous command. This alleviates confusion; with the Release he knows when he's done.

Teaching Watch Me

Training your Dachsie can be very difficult if you can't get him to pay attention to you. Most dogs will focus on their owner at home, but when out in public, they want to pay attention to everything but the owner! However, you can help your Dachsie succeed by teaching him how to pay attention with the *Watch me* command.

Again, sit or kneel down with your Dachsie or lift him up so you're both about the same height. With your Dachsie sitting in front of you and with treats in one hand, tell your dog, "Sweetie-pie, Watch me!" At the same time, let him sniff the treat and take it up to your chin. This movement and position is important. Let the dog sniff the treat so he knows you have it and then take it up to your chin (slowly) so you that as he watches the treat, his eyes follow your hand to your face.

Dog Talk
Watch me means your Dachsie should ignore distractions and look at your face, preferably making eye contact, and wait for your next command.

As he looks at the treat and then your face, praise him. After you praise him, "Good boy to Watch me!," pop the treat in his mouth quickly. Timing is important here; make sure you praise and reward him for looking at you. If he gets distracted and looks away, take the treat back to his nose and get his attention back to you.

> **Dachsie Wisdom**
>
> Use a treat your Dachsie really likes and then keep that treat just for training so it remains special.

As the dog learns the command, you can start making it more challenging. Tell your dog "Sweetie-pie, Watch me!" and then back away from your dog so he has to watch you while walking. When he can follow you for a few steps, make it more exciting by backing up in a zigzag pattern, making turns and corners. Back up quickly, then slowly. Add some challenges. Make sure you praise and reward him enthusiastically as you do this.

Eventually, you will combine the Watch me with the Heel command, which teaches the dog to walk nicely on the leash. However, the Heel is much easier for the dog to do if he can do a good Watch me. So practice the Watch me diligently for a while before teaching the Heel.

Teaching Lie Down

As with teaching the Sit command, sit or kneel on the ground with your Dachsie or lift him up on the furniture. Have your Dachsie sit. With a treat in one hand and another hand on the dog's shoulder, tell him "Sweetie-pie, Lie down," as you let him sniff the treat. Take the treat directly to the ground in front of his front paws. (Lead his nose down with the treat.) As he starts to move

> **Dog Talk**
>
> **Lie down** means to lower both hips and shoulders and get comfortable. He can lie on his chest, over on one side, or even on his back, as long as he's down and still.

down, the hand on his shoulder can be assisting him in this downward movement. However, don't try to push him down! If you push, he may simply push back. When he's down, give him the treat and praise him.

Use a treat and your hands to shape your Dachsie into a Down.

If your Dachsie didn't understand the significance of following the treat and remained in a Sit, you can help shape him into the Lie down position. Tell him "Sweetie-pie, Lie down," as you gently scoop his front legs up and out, shaping him into the Lie down. You can do this by reaching over his shoulders with one arm to grasp the front leg that's farthest from you while your other hand grasps the closest leg. Gently lift both legs up, forward, and then down.

> **Watch Out!**
> Don't let your Dachsie turn this into a wrestling contest. If he starts to thrash around, use your voice, "Acckk!" and use your hands to make him lie down.

The Down Is Comfy!

The Lie down command is very useful, both in the house and out in public, but also gives your Dachsie a chance to relax. Yes, he has to be still, but it doesn't take any effort to do so. When you practice the Down, you will use it in conjunction with the Stay command, which we'll teach next.

- Have your Dachsie lie down while you and other family members eat so he isn't begging under the table. Place him where you can see him but away from the table.

- Have him lie down at your feet while talking to guests. He can't be jumping all over them or knocking their drinks over if he's being still at your feet.

- Have him lie down and give him a toy to chew on when you would like to have some quiet time to read or watch television. Don't allow him to monopolize all your quiet time.

- Have your Dachsie lie down while you're talking to a neighbor.

- Have him lie down while you get your mail out of the box and sort through it.

As you practice with this command, you will find other ways to use it. For example, have your dog lie down in the bathroom while you're taking a shower; he can't get into trouble in another room if he's there with you. The important thing is that you use the command; find out where it can help you with your dog, and then use it.

Bet You Didn't Know

The Lie down command is a good exercise to help establish the owner's leadership position. Have your dog do at least one Lie down (although more is better) every single day.

Teaching Stay

The Sit and Lie down commands by themselves teach your Dachsie to hold the respective position (Sit or Lie down) until you release him, but only while you remain next to him. With the *Stay* command, you'll be able to walk away from him.

Begin in your training position, either kneeling down with your Dachsie, or with him up on the furniture. Have your dog sit. Hold your open palm in front of his face about two inches from his nose.

Dog Talk

Stay means "remain in this particular position while I walk away, and remain here until I come back to you and release you."

Tell him "Sweetie-pie, Stay!" Take a step or two away. If he moves, use your voice, "Acckk!" and put him back in position. Wait a few seconds and then step back to him. Have him hold still while you praise and pet him, then release him with the Release command.

If your dog is particularly wiggly, use the leash while you teach him. Have your dog sit. Hold your hand in front of his nose and tell him "Sweetie-pie, Stay!" In one hand, hold the leash up from his neck, slightly backward, without holding it tight. Take a step away while you continue to hold the leash up. If he moves, tell him "Acckk!" as you give him a slight snap and release correction with the leash. Put him back in position. Wait a few seconds, then step back to him, praise him, then release him.

After practicing the Stay with the Sit, try it with the Lie down. The training methods are the same, except you will be having the dog lie down. However, *you* tell the dog which to do. If you ask him to Sit-Stay and he decides to lie down, correct him and help him back up into a Sit. He doesn't get to choose which exercise; you do.

Stop That Whirling Dervish!

Use the Stay command around the house in conjunction with Sit and Lie down to control your Dachsie when he might normally get a little overexcited or overstimulated, such as in the following situations:

🏠 When you want him to stay away from the table while you're eating, have him lie down and tell him Stay.

🏠 Tell him to sit and stay while you're fixing his dinner so he doesn't jump all over you and spill his food.

🏠 When guests come over, have your Dachsie lie down by your feet and tell him Stay. He cannot then be tormenting your guests!

🏠 Have him sit and stay at doorways, gates, and at the curb so you can teach him to wait for permission.

There are lots of uses for these commands. Just look at your house, your routine, and where you might be having some problems with your dog's behavior. Where can the Stay help you?

Teaching Come

The *Come* command is very important, and one that could potentially save your Dachsie's life some day. When I teach my dogs to Come when called, I want them to understand that Come means "stop what you're doing and come back to me right now, with no hesitation, as fast as you can run." This instant response might save your dog from a dangerous situation—perhaps a dog fight, being hit by a car, or a snake in the grass. Situations come up every day that could cause your dog harm; a good response to the Come command could save him.

Dog Talk

You want your Dachsie to understand that **Come** means he should stop everything to come directly to you, right away, with no hesitation and no detours!

Because the Come command is so important, I will demonstrate a couple different techniques. Don't just focus on one technique; instead, practice both. Each technique teaches your Dachsie something different about the command.

The First Technique

Take a small plastic container, like a margarine container, and put a handful of dry kibble dog food in it. Put the top back on. If you shake it, you will hear a nice rattling sound. With your dog sitting in front of you, have the shaker in one hand and some good treats in the other. Shake the shaker and then pop a treat in his mouth.

Hard dog training, huh? What you are doing is teaching your Dachsie that the sound means he will get a treat, just like he recognizes the sound of his food in his bowl.

After two or three days of this training, you will add the word "Come." Start with your dog sitting in front of you (he's not going or coming anywhere); shake the shaker, say "Sweetie-pie, Come!" and pop the treat in his mouth. Now you're changing the equation. The sound of the shaker equals the word "Come," which equals the treat popped in his mouth! Practice this for several days, two or three times per session. Remember to use a happy tone of voice when you say "Come."

If you practice every day, by the end of the week start backing away from your Dachsie as you say "Sweetie-pie, Come!" Lead him by the nose with the treat as you back away. After a few steps, pop the treat in his mouth and praise him, "Good boy to Come!"

In a week or two, depending on how enthusiastic your dog is, you can stop having him sit in front of you. Instead, when he's across the room from you, pick up the shaker, call him, and when he charges across the room to you, praise him and pop the treat in his mouth.

The Second Technique

Put the leash on your Dachsie and hold the leash in one hand while you have some treats in the other. Back away from your dog as you call him, "Sweetie-pie, Come!" Make sure you back up a few steps so he gets a chance to chase you. If he doesn't come to you right away, use the leash to make sure he does. Praise him when he does come to you, "Good boy to Come!" and pop a treat in his mouth.

The Come command is very important.

The leash gives you control so you can ensure your Dachsie does come to you every time you call him. That means you have to use the leash when training him using this technique. If you know there are certain circumstances where your Dachsie gets distracted and ignores you, set him up! Make sure he's wearing the leash the next time so you can grab the leash or step on the end of it and make your dog come to you when you call him.

One of the most common mistakes dog owners make is they let their young dog have too much freedom too soon. If you let your dog run without his leash in the park, at the beach, or in a dog park and he will not come to you when you call him, you have a problem. Every time you beg him to come and he ignores you, you teach him that you don't have control. Dogs, especially Dachsies, are smart enough to learn this.

Therefore, while your dog is young, in training, and while he still needs to learn to come better, make sure he's on a leash or a long line (20 or 30 feet of clothesline rope) while he's outside of the fenced back yard. Watch him, of course, to make sure the long line or leash doesn't get tangled while he's playing. And in the yard, always take the leash off him when you cannot supervise him.

> **Watch Out!**
> Never correct your dog for anything to do with the Come. Timing is vitally important, and if he misunderstands a correction, he could learn that coming to you is bad and results in a correction.

> **Watch Out!**
> Don't call your dog to come and do anything he dislikes (a bath, for example). Make the Come positive and fun *all* the time!

If your Dachsie is off his leash and hesitates about coming to you—especially if something is distracting him, you might be able to trick him to come to you. First, don't chase him. That will only make him run farther and faster away from you. Instead, call his name in an exciting (not scolding) tone of voice and then run away from him. He will turn and chase after you!

Teaching Let's Go

With your dog on the leash and the end of the leash held in one hand, let your Dachsie sniff the treat you have in your other hand,

> **Dog Talk**
> Let's go! means your Dachsie should walk with you on the leash in no particular position, but should respect the leash without fighting it, pulling on it, or choking himself on it.

and tell him "Sweetie-pie, Watch me! Let's go!" and simply back away from him. If he watches you, praise him and give him the treat. If he follows you, praise him even more. However, if he sniffs the ground, looks away from you, or tries to pull the other direction, use a snap and release of the leash and a verbal correction, "Acckk! No pull!" (Or no sniff, if that's appropriate.) After the correction, if he looks back up to you, praise him.

Only walk four or five steps in the beginning. This takes concentration on your dog's part, and you want to set him up to succeed. As his concentration gets better, you can increase the number of steps you walk.

As he gets better, too, you can make it more challenging. Back away from the dog several times in several different directions. Each time he follows you and each time he looks up at you, praise him and give him a treat. Every time he pulls away, sniffs the ground, or ignores you, correct him.

When your Dachsie is following you well as you back away, begin turning so you are both walking in the same direction. If your dog dashes past you to pull forward, simply make an about-face turn so you are going the opposite direction. Without saying anything to your dog, just hold the leash securely, turn, and go. Your dog will hit the end of the leash as you turn, and when he does, act surprised, "Wow! What happened?" When he turns to go with you, praise him. However, if he dashes past you again, turn around again, repeating the entire exercise.

You may have to go back and forth a few times. However, pretty soon he's going to figure out that it's to his advantage to pay attention to where you are walking and to go with you.

Your goal—with either method—is to have your dog keep the leash slack as he follows you, paying attention to your every move. And of course, when he does, you will praise him enthusiastically!

Dachsie Wisdom

As you train your dog, watch his eyes and ears; he'll tell you whether he's alert and eager to do these things (his body language will be up and forward) or whether he's worried (body language will be down and slinky).

Teaching Heel

Teaching the *Heel* requires a great deal of concentration on your dog's part. Do *not* start teaching the Heel until your dog has been following the Watch me command for several weeks (not days, weeks!) and has been obeying the Let's go command very well for at least two weeks with regular practice.

Begin with your dog on leash, and hold the leash in your left hand and some treats in the right. Back away from your dog as you tell him, "Sweetie-pie, Let's go!" As he follows you, let him catch up with you as you back up slightly and turn so you are facing the direction he is walking and he ends up on your left side. Walk forward together as you show him a treat and tell him, "Sweetie-pie, Heel!" Stop after just a few steps, have him sit, and praise him as you give him the treat.

Dog Talk

To your Dachsie, **Heel** will come to mean, "walk by my left side with your neck and shoulder area next to my left leg, maintaining that position no matter what I do."

Repeat this several times, keeping each walking session short, enthusiastic, and fun. Make it challenging by turning, walking fast, walking slow, and going different directions.

At this point in the training, always start with the "Let's go!" command and tell the dog to heel as he arrives at your left side and you begin walking forward together.

When you can both do this well, have your dog sit by your left side, on leash, and hold the leash in your left hand. Have some treats in your right hand. Show the dog a treat and tell him, "Sweetie-pie, Watch me!" When he's paying attention to you, tell him, "Sweetie-pie, Heel!" and walk forward. If he pulls ahead, use the leash to give him a snap and release correction as you tell him, "Acckk! No pull!" When he slows down, backs off the pulling, and looks back to you, praise him and repeat the Watch me command. When he watches you, praise him enthusiastically.

Again, make sure you keep the sessions short and upbeat and praise the dog's successes.

When you take your dog for a walk, don't ask him to heel the entire way. Instead, go back and forth between Let's go and Heel. Offer some variety and some challenge. However, once you start this training, do not let your dog pull on the leash—*ever!* Whenever he is on the leash, he should respect it and never, ever be allowed to pull on it.

Watch Out!
Dogs who pull on their leash risk damaging their neck, so never allow your Dachsie to pull on the leash.

Some Tips for Successful Training Sessions

My dogs love their training sessions. When I get out the leashes, collars, and other training equipment, all three dogs shove each other aside so that one can sit nicely right in front of me. If they could talk, they would be telling me, "I'm sitting nicely! Pick me! Pick me!"

Some people look on training as work—something to do to their dogs—but I look upon this as something my dogs and I do together. We're friends, a good team, and enjoy the time we spend together—even training. How do I keep them excited about training? I do the following:

🏠 I keep the training sessions fun. Even when we have a difficult session or have a lot to learn, I keep it as upbeat as possible with verbal praise, food treats, or other motivators. I'm not embarrassed to clap my hands and jump up and down as I praise my dogs' efforts.

🏠 I look upon it as my job to communicate what I want to my dogs. That means I need to let the dog know what I want him to do, when I want him to do it, and how. If my dog is having trouble, rather than think of it as his problem, I think of it as mine! I need look at my communications with him and fix it.

- If my dog is confused, I never hesitate to go back to the very basics of an exercise, reteach it, and try to see where the confusion set in. If my dog is confused, I see it as my fault for not making the lesson clear.

- I watch my dog's body language, and when the dog is stressed (yawning, ears and lips pulled back, drooling, laying down, or refusing to work), I stop training for the moment and give the dog a massage or tummy rub. While giving the tummy rub, I rethink my training and try to see where I stressed out my dog. How can I get around that roadblock?

- I picture myself as a fair, kind, caring, but firm trainer. I keep training sessions fun, but the dogs do have to pay attention to me and I will always enforce my rules. My dogs are well loved but are not spoiled rotten.

- I intersperse play with training. We'll train for a few minutes, then play. We'll train a little more, then play. This keeps the fun level high and the dogs' interest up.

- I practice all our commands in the house, in the yard, in the car, and out in public. I want to make sure my dogs understand the rules are in effect *all* the time; not just during training sessions.

So don't forget when you're training your Dachsie to be consistent, to be in control, and to always make sure you're both having fun.

The Least You Need to Know

- All dogs should learn the eight basic obedience commands—including Dachshunds!

- Teach your dog the eight basic commands—Come, Sit, Release, Lie down, Stay, Watch me, Let's go, and Heel—and learn to use them in your daily routine.

- Keep your training session fun, upbeat, but under control.

- Don't just hope your training sessions are successful; do everything you can to make them successful!

Chapter 16

Dachshunds Make Mistakes Sometimes

In This Chapter

🏠 Why Dachshunds get into trouble

🏠 What we do to cause problems

🏠 Dealing with a barking Dachsie

🏠 Some common behavior problems and solutions

🏠 Suggestions for handling other problems

Dachshunds like to bark. Unfortunately, not everyone—especially neighbors—likes to listen to Dachsies bark! In my training classes, I always ask new students what problem behaviors they would like to focus on during their training and, invariably, Dachshund owners say, "Barking!" Dachsies bark to warn of people walking down the street, approaching the house, or in the yards next door. Dachsies bark when another dog is nearby, when the neighbor's cat is on the fence, or when a bird flutters overhead. Dachsies bark!

Although in our close neighborhoods today, this barking is more of a problem than a positive thing, it was originally very much a part of the Dachshund's hunting heritage. The barking had a purpose. Today, although watchdogs still have a place in our society, constant uncontrollable barking is a problem.

Luckily, even barking Dachsies can learn to control themselves. Luckily, too, most Dachsies are not problem dogs. Dachsies can learn more socially acceptable behavior once you learn how and why Dachsies do what they do!

Why Does He Do That?

Most behaviors we consider problems are not problems to the dog. Dachsies bark because they have something to say; they are communicating, just as we speak. Keep in mind some people talk too much, just as some dogs bark too much. Furthermore, Dachsies dig because they love to hunt. Your backyard may not have badgers, but there may be gophers, mice, bugs, or just a host of good smells. But there are other things that affect problem behavior; sometimes quite significantly.

Are You the Leader?

We have talked previously in this book about the importance of leadership—your leadership. Because Dachshunds had to be tough and tenacious to be the hunting dogs they were designed to be, they'll assume the family leadership if you aren't a strong leader. However, doing so is not emotionally healthy for your dog, and a dog without a leader can develop a host of behavior problems, including leg-lifting, marking, mounting, humping, and other unacceptable behaviors. Aggressive behavior toward family members is common, as is destructive behavior around the house. Food guarding, toy guarding, and similar behaviors are also common for dogs without leaders.

Some dog owners initially feel that they are being mean when trying to assume a leadership position. These people usually want their dog for companionship and want their dog to love them as much as they love their dog. Unfortunately, a relationship between a dog—especially a strong-willed dog—and a person isn't always that easy.

Love and affection without assertiveness is usually regarded by the dog as weakness. With most Dachsies, love and affection must also be accompanied by respect. If your Dachsie doesn't respect you, you will be looked on as weak. Unfortunately, then that love and affection you want your Dachsie to give you will also be lacking. So be tough, even if you really don't want to be, and that love and affection you are looking for will be there as your dog also learns to respect you.

Don't allow your dog to engage you in a power struggle. If he argues with you, use his leash and collar to help him do what you want. Never, ever allow him to use his strength against you; it would be too easy for him to win. Even a small dog can injure a person.

Watch Out!
If your Dachsie is an adult and thinks he's the leader and you are trying to change things, be careful. If you even *think* you could be bitten, hire a trainer or behaviorist to help you.

Is Your Dachsie Healthy?

Well-trained and well-adjusted dogs usually don't begin bad behaviors for no reason; there's usually something that triggers it. If your dog has been well-housetrained and suddenly begins having accidents in the house, make an appointment with your veterinarian. Often a urinary tract infection will cause housetraining accidents. Other health concerns can trigger problem behavior, too, so a thorough exam is always a good idea.

Dachsie Wisdom
Many behaviorists and dog trainers feel that at least 20 percent of all behavior problems are related to the dog's health in some way.

Bet You Didn't Know

Medications can have side effects that show up in behavior. If your dog has recently started a new medication and his behavior has changed, talk to your veterinarian.

When you make your appointment and when you see the veterinarian, make sure you tell him you are going to be working on some problem behaviors and want to pinpoint or eliminate any potential health problems. Don't just ask for an exam and leave the vet guessing as to why he's examining your dog!

Is Life Interesting?

Dachshunds were bred to do a job—to help the farmer rid his farm of pests and predators. If your Dachsie is a pet, living in your house with you, many years of hunting instincts are now sitting idle. Oh, he may chase the occasional bird in the backyard or hunt the field mouse that sneaks into the garage, but that's nothing like a regular job. You know that old saying, "Idle hands are the devil's workshop." Idle paws are, too!

A bored Dachsie is going to get into trouble. What he does may vary—many bark, some dig, and some chew. You need to figure out how to alleviate some of this boredom.

- Increase his exercise so he's more likely to sleep when left alone.
- Keep his obedience skills sharp; this challenges his mind.
- Get involved in a dog sport or activity so he has something else to occupy his mind and body.
- If he gets into trouble when left alone, give him a toy before you leave—a rawhide, a biscuit, or a small paper bag with treats in it.
- If you are gone for long hours during the day, hire a dog walker, a neighbor, or the neighbor's teenage daughter to come over and spend some time with your dog while you're at work.

Is Your Dachsie's Food Right for Him?

Dachsies aren't normally demanding about their food; many will thrive on just about any food. However, some dog foods that are more than 50 percent carbohydrates are known to cause a type of hyperactivity in some dogs—including Dachsies. Foods high in some sugars and starches also cause behavior problems in some dogs. Many dogs are also very sensitive to some food coloring, preservatives, or other additives.

If you suspect a food-related problem, read the label of the food you are feeding. Most Dachshunds do very well on a dry kibble food that has between 25 and 30 percent carbohydrates. Make sure most of the carbohydrates are from sources other than cereal grains. For examples, potatoes, sweet potatoes, and blueberries are a better source of carbohydrates than cereal grains are.

Feed your Dachsie a food that doesn't contain a lot of sugar and artificial preservatives, colorings, and additives.

Dachsie Wisdom

If you switch foods, take your time. Add a little of the new food to the old and gradually—over two weeks—add more of the new food until finally your serving him only the new food.

Is Your Dachsie a Couch Potato?

Lack of exercise causes many problems. A Dachsie who hasn't gotten enough exercise may—literally—bounce off the walls! A young healthy dog needs to run, explore, and use up his energy. If he doesn't get a chance to do that, he's likely to do it in the house. Or he's going to do something else to use up some of that energy, and that may include pacing, digging, barking, or some other destructive behavior.

Bet You Didn't Know

Just as people are getting more sedentary, so are our dogs. Experts say that more people are overweight today than at any time during recorded history, and veterinarians say the same thing about our dogs. An overweight dog is neither happy nor healthy. Regular aerobic exercise can help use up your dog's excess energy and can help keep his weight at a healthy level.

Dachsie Wisdom

The amount of exercise needed will vary from dog to dog. A nice quarter-mile walk around the neighborhood would be enough for a three- to four-month-old Dachsie puppy, but a two-mile jog would be better for a full grown, healthy adult Dachsie.

A dog who doesn't get enough exercise can have other problems, including health problems.

Dachshunds do, unfortunately, tend to get chubby. An overweight Dachsie may also end up with more back problems. A slim Dachsie is a healthier Dachsie and a happier Dachsie!

How Old Is Your Dachsie?

Dachshund temperament can change depending on the dog's age. For example, most Dachsie puppies go through a slight challenging stage between four and five months of age. One moment the puppy may be normal and bold, and the next moment he may be biting your hands. The next day, the puppy may be afraid of his own shadow. This is normal for this age, though, and is nothing to be worried about. Some of the worst things you can do are baby the puppy, shelter him, or get too rough with him. Instead, keep life calm, on schedule, and continue with your training.

Another bad stage is adolescence. Most Dachsies go into adolescence between 6 and 12 months of age, most typically between 7 and 9 months. An adolescent dog is very much like a human teenager. They are trying to be grown up and independent and will push your limits to see if you are going to enforce the rules. Again, don't get excited. Just enforce your rules and do your training.

Some Dachsies, especially females, have a bad stage again at about two years of age. These Dachsies think they are grown up and quite important. This is when your leadership skills become very important. If you are not the leader now, this is when your Dachsie will try to take over. This is a very key time to review those leadership skills, make sure you are doing them, and enforce your training.

Dachsies often get into trouble when lonely or bored, so use playtime to overcome both.

What We Do to Our Dogs

As a dog obedience instructor, I watch dogs and their owners every day. I watch how dog owners interact with their dogs, and I marvel at how well dogs get along in our world in spite of us! Unfortunately, we—the owners of dogs—are often the cause of behavior problems. And worse yet, the problems caused by the owners are the hardest to solve, because it is harder to see problems within ourselves than it is to see the problems in our dogs.

Some of the most common problems caused by the owners include the following:

- Overemotional owners who are quick to get excited or quick to react often end up with dogs just like them. Unfortunately, during episodes of excitement, these dogs can get out of hand. Dachshunds, being quick, reactive dogs anyway, often become uncontrollable with an owner like this.

- Overprotective owners take away the dog's ability to cope with the world around him. By protecting him from everything, such owners cause the dog to become fearful, sometimes aggressively fearful. When I see a shy, timid Dachsie, I always wonder what has happened to him, because this breed is not known to be shy.

- Overly permissive owners don't set enough rules or, when they do set rules, they don't enforce them. These owners are not the dog's leader, and many problem behaviors can develop.

- Shy, timid owners tend to have dogs with one of two personalities. Many timid people end up with a loud, extroverted dog who can portray his bolder self. This dog may become overprotective of his timid owner, sometimes dangerously. Or the shy owner may get a dog just like himself, and the two will go through life very quietly.

- Demanding owners would prefer the dog to be a furry robot who follows each and every order exactly as given. Dogs, of course, will make mistakes. Dachsies belonging to these owners will never measure up, no matter how hard they try. In addition, Dachshunds were simply not bred to be furry robots; they think too much, and an owner trying to turn a Dachsie into a robot will be sorely disappointed.

- Mean owners overpower their dogs and make their dogs fearful or fearfully aggressive. Because aggression begets aggression in certain dogs, these owners often wind up with a dog as mean as they are. Dachshunds may be small, but a mean one is just as dangerous as a mean dog of any other breed.

Changing Problem Behavior

Changing problem behavior requires a commitment from you. You are going to have to be involved in the process, and that may require you to make some changes. You may have to make some physical changes around the house or yard, or you may have to adjust your daily schedule. If you make the effort, however, your chances of success are greatly increased. Most canine behavior problems can be changed, and if not cured, at least controlled.

Let's start at the beginning:

🏠 Make sure your Dachsie is healthy. Don't assume he is healthy; make an appointment with your veterinarian and tell your vet why you are there.

🏠 Make sure your Dachsie gets enough vigorous exercise. This does not mean time running around the house or yard, but good, vigorous, aerobic exercise.

🏠 Make and keep a regular schedule for training. Fifteen minutes of Sit, Lie down, Stay, Heel, and Come—all on leash—will help keep his skills sharp and his mind attentive.

🏠 Incorporate the training into your daily routine. Make your Dachsie sit for everything and have him do a down stay each day. Have him sit and stay at open doors.

🏠 Make the time for play, and have fun with your dog. The time spent with you is important, but so is laughter!

🏠 Prevent problems from occurring when you can. Put away the trash cans, pick up the children's toys, and put away the lawn furniture cushions.

Bet You Didn't Know

Preventing problems from occurring might mean limiting your Dachsie's freedom. Don't let him have free run of the house, and supervise him more closely.

🏠 Teach your Dachsie an *alternative behavior*. He can't jump on you if he learns to sit for petting. He can't dash out the front door if he has been taught to sit and wait at the door.

Dog Talk

An **alternative behavior** is one that your Dachsie can do and be praised for while at the same time it prevents another behavior from happening for which he might be corrected.

🏠 Set your Dachsie up to learn. Arrange things so he makes a mistake when you're there to teach him. Use your training skills to teach him.

Exercise can use up excess energy that can cause problem behavior.

Common Problems and Solutions

Every dog—even every dog of the same breed—is different from others in some way. Although most Dachshunds are tenacious, some are softer or more sensitive to training than others. This affects how the dog should be trained and how problem behaviors should be handled. However, over the years, I have found a few methods that seem to work well for most Dachsies.

Barking Is a Problem

Dachsies bark for a number of reasons. Protective dogs bark to warn you of trespassers—real or imagined. Social dogs bark to communicate with you and the world around them. Dogs bark at the kids playing out front, the birds flying overhead, and the neighbor's dog barking down the block. Unfortunately, a barking dog is also a nuisance; sometimes a major nuisance.

Start correcting barking in the house when you are close. Make up a squirt bottle with about ⅛ white vinegar and the rest water. (You want just enough vinegar so you can smell it.) When someone comes to the door, for example, and your dog barks, walk quietly to the dog, tell him, "Quiet!" firmly but without yelling. Mist the vinegar water toward him. He will smell the vinegar, stop barking, back off, and maybe even sneeze. When he stops barking, tell him, "Good boy to be quiet!"

Watch Out!

Make sure the solution is primarily water with just a little vinegar—⅛ vinegar to ⅞ water is good. A stronger mixture could sting your dog's eyes. Also, use the squirt bottle on mist setting, not stream. A hard stream setting could hurt your dog if you hit him in the face or eyes.

If you yell at your dog to stop barking (most people's first reaction), you're doing the same thing he's doing—making lots of noise at the front door. To your dog, you're barking, too! So of course, he isn't going to stop, he thinks you're the reinforcements!

However, when you quietly tell him to be quiet as you spray this nasty-smelling vinegar water, he hears the command as you make it difficult for him to continue barking. Dachsies have a sensitive sense of smell, and very few dogs enjoy the smell of vinegar. Make sure you praise him for being quiet when he does stop barking. You don't want to just correct; you must also tell him what is right.

Once your dog has learned what the word *quiet* means, start asking him to be quiet in other situations. Whenever he starts to bark inappropriately, tell him to be quiet, and make sure you back up your command. Again, always praise him for being quiet when he does.

If your dog barks when you're not home, you may have to set up a situation so you can catch him in the act. Go through all the motions of leaving: Get dressed; pick up your purse, wallet, or briefcase; get in the car; and drive down the block. Park the car down the block and walk back with squirt bottle in hand. When your dog starts to bark, surprise him with a "Quiet!" and a squirt! If you set him up a few times, he will quickly learn that you have much more control than he thought!

Dachsie Wisdom

A distraction also works for many "home alone" barkers. Give him a Buster Cube or Kong (food-dispensing toys) before you leave, and he won't even know you've left!

I don't recommend most of the electronic anti-bark collars for most Dachsies. If you feel you have a serious barking problem and would like to try one of these collars, call a trainer or behaviorist for help first. You shouldn't have to hurt your Dachsie to train him.

However, one new collar on the market has worked very well for some Dachsies. This collar, instead of administering a shock, squirts out a burst of citronella spray. Working on the same principle as the vinegar squirt bottle, it offends the Dachsie's sense of smell, stopping the barking, usually in mid-bark!

Because Dachsies do have a tendency to be barkers, changing this habit takes time, consistency in training, and patient neighbors. Make sure you talk to your neighbors and tell them you are trying to control the situation.

Dachsies Do Jump!

Dachsie's short legs don't keep them from jumping up on people. Some owners don't seem to mind, but even a short-legged Dachsie can scratch skin, rip clothes, and knock over children. In addition, most Dachshund experts agree Dachsies should not jump on people because it risks damaging the Dachsie's back!

To stop him from jumping up on people, teach your Dachsie to sit (see Chapter 15). This may seem very simple, but when the dog learns to sit for attention, including petting from you, he will sit in front of you, quivering in anticipation of petting, and will have no need to jump on you. If you consistently reward him for sitting, the jumping behavior will disappear.

You will also have to teach him to sit for other people. Use his leash and simply do not allow him to jump up. Have him sit first (before people greet him) and then when he tries to jump, use a snap and release correction as you tell him, "No jump!" Make him sit, and ask other people not to pet him until he's sitting.

Watch Out! Teaching your dog to sit instead of jumping up requires consistency in training. Everyone must make sure the dog sits; if someone is inconsistent, the dog will continue to jump up.

Destructive Chewing

You may be relieved to find out that destructive chewing isn't a hard problem to solve if you follow a few careful guidelines:

🏠 First, consistently correct the Dachsie each and every time he puts his mouth on something he shouldn't. Follow up each and every correction by handing him one of his toys. You show him what's wrong: "No! That's mine." Take the wrong item away as you tell him, "Here, this is your toy. Good boy!" and hand him his toy.

🏠 Prevent chewing problems from happening as much as possible. Never allow your dog to have unsupervised access to stuff that can be destroyed.

🏠 Don't let him have free run of the house—close bedroom doors, put up baby gates, and keep him close.

🏠 Never assume that your puppy or young dog knows what he can chew and what he can't. Never give your puppy something to chew now that you won't want him to chew later. He'll understand later—that's why you're teaching him now.

Watch Out!

Destructive chewing isn't just a bad habit; it can threaten your dog's life should he chew on the wrong thing. Make sure anything that is poisonous is locked up away from your dog.

🏠 Walk around the house, yard, and garage with your dog. What strikes his interest? What does he want to get into? How can you prevent him from destroying those things? Be proactive and stop it from happening before it actually does!

Digging

As hunters who would normally go down a hole after their prey, many Dachsies are enthusiastic diggers. Luckily, however, many will not start a hole on their own, although they might enlarge a hole, such as a gopher hole! However, some Dachsies just seem to like to dig and will do so enthusiastically!

Prevent your Dachsie from sneaking off to get into trouble.

Most digging happens when the owner isn't at home. Rarely does it happen when you're there to witness it, and that's too bad because to correct it, you have to catch the dog in the act. Correcting him later, when you come home and discover it, does not work.

To stop the digging, you will need to prevent it from happening as much as possible. When you're not home, don't let the Dachsie have free access to the lawn and gardens. Build him a dog run where he can do anything he wants! Then, when you're at home, you can let him run around the back yard and when you see him start to dig (or sniff the gopher holes) you can interrupt and teach him. "Acckk! No dig!"

To show your Dachsie the place where he can dig, find a spot in the yard, perhaps behind the garage or in an out-of-the-way corner, where you can dig up the soil. Using a shovel, loosen the dirt really well. Take half a dozen dog biscuits and stick them in the dirt so they are only partially covered. Invite your dog to find the biscuits and to dig here. As he finds the biscuits, completely bury a few so he has to dig for them, and in the beginning, help him do so. For the first few days, continue to bury something in this spot and invite him to find it. When he digs elsewhere, correct him and take him back to his spot; he'll learn.

Mouthing and Biting

Although it is very natural for your dog to use his mouth in play or to make you do (or stop doing) something—after all, he doesn't have any hands!—biting can't be allowed for any reason. It only takes one bite for authorities to confiscate your dog and kill him. No aggressive intent must be proved, either. Legally, a bite is a bite no matter what the dog's intent. That means if your Dachsie tries to play rough with the neighbor kids while they are running and playing with your kids in your backyard, and he nips one of the kids on the back of the leg, that is considered a bite even though no vicious intent may have been displayed.

> **Watch Out!**
>
> If your dog bites someone, not only can your dog be killed, but depending on where you live, you can also face a lawsuit from the victim, medical costs, criminal charges, a fine, and possibly even jail time!

The Center for Disease Control in Atlanta, Georgia, has declared a dog-bite epidemic, saying that more than 800,000 dog bite cases are reported yearly. When you consider that these are only the bites requiring medical attention, the numbers of actual bites are probably two to three times this number.

Every dog must learn that touching teeth to skin or clothing is absolutely forbidden. Ideally, you should start teaching these lessons when your Dachsie is a puppy, but even older puppies and adult dogs can learn.

- Be consistent. Don't allow your Dachsie to bite you during play and then correct him for nipping in other situations.

- Don't play games that teach him to use his strength against you. No tug-of-war and no wrestling.

- Don't allow the dog to chase the children, and don't allow him to play rough with the kids, nipping at their heels or clothing.

- Teach the children to play quietly with the dog; no running and screaming.

- Don't allow your Dachsie to grab at his leash, chew on it, mouth it, or pull against it with the leash in his mouth.

There are several ways to correct mouthing and biting. No one of these corrections is better or worse than the others; some are more usable in certain situations.

Use the squirt bottle (⅛ vinegar to ⅞ water) for those instances where the dog is nipping at your legs, heels, or clothes. Have the squirt bottle in hand in those situations (or times) when you know he is apt to do it. When he nips at your heels, squirt him as you tell him, "No bite!" When he backs off, praise him quietly, "Good boy."

If you have your hands on your dog, perhaps when hooking up his leash, playing with him, or petting him, and he tries to mouth or bite you, correct him right away without hesitation. With one hand, grab his buckle collar or the scruff of his neck (as a handle) and with the other hand simply close his mouth. Tell him firmly, "No bite!" Do not let go of his muzzle until he takes a deep sigh and relaxes. If you let go and he continues to try and mouth or bite you, close his mouth again, correct him again, and wait him out.

Bet You Didn't Know _____

A temper tantrum is when your Dachsie (usually a puppy) protests something you're doing to him by throwing himself around, crying, growling, or screaming, and often, by trying to bite you. A temper tantrum in a puppy is bad behavior on his part. Do not give in. If he wanted you to stop brushing him, for example, when the tantrum is over, continue brushing him!

Dachsie Wisdom ___

Make sure you praise your dog when he doesn't put his mouth on you in situations where he might have done so prior to your training. Remember, corrections tell the dog when he made a mistake, but praise shows him what to continue doing!

When you're teaching him, don't lose your temper. Aggression begets aggression, and if you get angry and lose your temper, your dog may very well retaliate. If you lose your temper often, his behavior may mirror your own, becoming more aggressive in response to you. When you correct puppy biting and mouthing, correct him fairly and firmly—just as you did any other behavior—without losing your temper.

Suggestions for Other Problems

Over time, there might be a few other things come up that you don't want to live with. If that happens, don't panic. Many behaviors can be changed or prevented with a minimum of fuss.

- **Digging under the fence.** Bury some rocks in the holes he digs under the fence and then try to figure out why he is digging under the fence. Are the neighborhood kids teasing him? Is there a dog on the other side of the fence? Make sure he's getting enough exercise, playtime, and attention from you.

- **Chasing cars, kids on in-line skates, bikes, and skateboards.**
  Keep him on leash and, when he tries to chase, correct him
  with the leash and have him sit. Enforce the Sit and Sit-Stay
  commands. If he can't sit still, turn around and walk the other
  direction; if he doesn't walk with you, let the leash correct
  him—*hard!* Praise him when he does walk with you.

- **Barking in the car.** Make him ride in the car in his kennel
  crate. He is safer that way, anyway, because the crate can be
  held in place with a seat belt. Then, have a squirt bottle handy
  and, when he barks, squirt him and tell him, "Quiet!"

Let's Review the Process

Thousands of dogs are given up by their owners to shelters every
year because of problem behaviors. This is tragic because so many
problems can be changed or controlled.

- Make sure you are your Dachsie's leader.

- Ask yourself why your Dachsie is doing something. Look at it
  from his point of view, not yours! Is he getting enough exercise?
  Are you spending enough time with him? Does he have a health
  problem that might be causing it? Are neighborhood kids teasing him outside the fence?

- Figure out the best way to teach him. Set him up so the problem will happen while you're at home and able to correct him.
  Make sure you praise him if he decides not to do it!

- If possible, prevent the problem from occurring in the first
  place. Will a dog run help? Or his kennel crate? Does your
  Dachsie need more supervision?

- Practice his obedience commands regularly, and use them around
  the house and yard. Incorporate them into your daily routine.

The Least You Need to Know

🏠 Problem behaviors usually happen for a reason. Try to find out why your dog is doing what he's doing.

🏠 Prevent problems from happening if you can, especially when you aren't there to teach him.

🏠 When you are at home, teach him what is wrong and, most important, teach him what is right!

🏠 You may have to make some changes to control problem behaviors.

Chapter 17

Why Does My Dachshund Do That?

In This Chapter

- 🏠 Understanding the canine body
- 🏠 Understanding hunting dog behavior
- 🏠 Looking at the strange things dogs do
- 🏠 Common questions and answers about dog behavior

Many first-time Dachshund owners ask why their dogs chase every-thing that moves or why their Dachsie likes to crawl under the bed covers. Others ask why their Dachshund loves to sleep in the dark cave under the foot of the reclining chair even after having been caught in it when the foot rest came down.

Other misunderstandings occur when dog owners see their dog do something that to them is quite disgusting (like eating cat feces). Because dog owners don't know why these behaviors happen, the behaviors can be the cause of a lot of confusion between dog and owner. Sometimes even the experts don't know why dogs do what they do; after all, the dog can't tell us. But we can make some educated guesses. This chapter will hopefully answer some of your questions.

Understanding Body Language

Dogs do use their voices to communicate—as we do—and most dog owners recognize their dog's own unique verbalizations in specific situations—a deep bark when the delivery man comes to the door, the happy yelps when you come home, and a whine when the dog needs to go outside. However, dogs also use their bodies to communicate. Body language is very rich in meaning, and you can learn a lot by watching how your Dachsie uses it.

Why Do Dogs Pant Even When They Aren't Hot?

Dogs pant to lose heat. With his big, wet tongue hanging out, a dog can lose a lot of heat through the evaporation process. Because dogs don't sweat anywhere except on the pads of their feet, this cooling process is very important.

However, panting is also a sign of stress. When in a situation that bothers him, for any reason, your Dachsie might begin to pant. If he anticipates something happening at the veterinarian's office, your dog may begin to pant even though the air conditioning is on in the office.

If you notice this type of panting during a training session, take the pressure off. Have him do something he can do well—such as sit—praise him for sitting and then take a break. Rub his tummy, throw the ball for a few minutes, and relax. Then go back to your training, but ease the pressure somewhat.

Why Does He Yawn When He's Not Tired?

Yawning when not sleepy is what is called a calming signal. If, during your training sessions, for example, your Dachsie looks away from you and yawns, he is trying to tell you to calm down. Apparently, he is feeling stress, either from himself or from you, and he's trying to relieve it. Other calming signals include eye blinking, sneezing, looking away, and scratching.

Many Dachsies will yawn when being scolded. You may be scolding your Dachsie about getting into the trash and your Dachsie will yawn at you. Essentially, he's telling you to mellow out, to calm down. Personally, I don't take this well. I have a tendency to get even more excited when my dogs tell me to calm down. How you react is up to you!

Why Does He Wag His Tail When He's Not Happy?

Although most people think a dog only wags his tail when he's happy, that isn't necessarily true. With most dogs, a wagging tail is a sign of emotion, usually strong emotions. Strong emotions—of which happiness is, of course, one—are expressed by the dog in various ways using his body language. For example, the dog will sink lower and crouch when he is feeling submissive or worried, and his posture will lift and move forward when he's feeling strong and dominant. A dog standing tall and stiff, wagging his tail slowly, may be aggressive.

With Dachsies, the dog's entire tail and back end will wiggle. Some Dachsies can get the entire hip section moving back and forth. With their tendency toward back problems, you might wonder why they wag so enthusiastically, but they do. The strength of the movement will depend on the emotions being portrayed, of course.

Why Does He Lower His Front End When He Wants Me to Play with Him?

When a Dachsie lowers his front end, including his head and shoulders, leaving his hips high, this is called a play bow. This body language is a natural expression of play and is used by dogs, wolves, coyotes, and many of the other canine species. Puppies will use this play invitation when they want their littermates to play with them, as well as with adult dogs and their human playmates, including you.

Bet You Didn't Know
If you want to invite your Dachsie to play, you can use the same body language. Lift your hands high, then bring them down in front of you, making a bowing motion.

Understanding the Dachsie Physique

The way dogs perceive the world and how they behave has a lot to do with how they are built. For example, we use our sense of sight for information about the world around us. Some dog breeds, including Greyhounds and other sighthounds, use vision, but many other breeds, including Dachsies, depend more on their senses of hearing and smell for information about the world.

Dachsie Wisdom
As hunting dogs, Dachsies use their sense of smell more than some other breeds. However, scent alone isn't the key; so is movement. Movement to a hunting dog signifies a pest that must be caught or a predator that should be chased away.

Certain physical characteristics also make dogs react in ways we don't understand. For example, their digestive systems often compel them to make choices that seem strange to us. In addition, their reproductive systems exert powerful forces on their behavior.

How Well Do Dachsies Smell?

We can't even imagine how well Dachsies smell the world around them. For example, we think salt is odorless, but a trained scenting dog can actually smell salt dissolved in water. This ability is why dogs are used so frequently by law enforcement agencies to detect drugs, illegal substances, bombs, and even poached animals and animal products.

Many Dachsies have earned tracking dog titles through the American Kennel Club. If your Dachsie likes to use his nose, you might want to consider this dog sport.

Scent is a very important sense for all Dachshunds.

If My Dachsie's Nose Is So Sensitive, Why Does He Roll in Stinky Stuff?

This is another habit that puzzles many dog owners. Why would an animal with such a sensitive nose roll itself in cow manure, rotting carcasses, or other stinky stuff? Although the dogs can't tell us why, some experts say that many predators, including dogs, roll in filth to help disguise their scent. Other experts say that the dog simply likes a particular scent—for whatever reason—because not every dog appears attracted to rotting carcasses. Some dogs will roll in cat urine, some will roll on tobacco products, and others appear to be attracted to petroleum products. Some dogs don't roll in anything! It seems to be a personal statement some dogs make.

Should I Let My Vet Spay My Dachsie?

Your veterinarian wants to spay your female Dachsie for several reasons. The first and most important to you are the health benefits. The chances of your dog getting any reproductive cancers later in life are drastically decreased if your Dachsie is spayed prior to her first season. Second, having a dog in season is not fun. Male dogs will come calling, and your dog will suddenly become an escape artist. Last, but certainly still important, there are too many Dachsies out there who need homes. The Dachsie rescue and adoption groups have more dogs to place than they can handle. Only the very best dogs need to be bred, and that means the best dogs as compared to their respective breed standards (see Chapter 2 for the Dachsie standard).

> **Bet You Didn't Know**
> Myths and old wives' tales aside, a female dog doesn't have to have a litter of puppies or go through a season before she's spayed. It is much healthier for her if she is spayed before those happen.

Why Should I Neuter My Male Dog?

A male should be neutered for many of the same reasons a female should be spayed. There are too many puppies being produced and then killed because there aren't enough homes for them all. Chances of cancers of the reproductive system are drastically decreased if he's been neutered. In addition, a neutered male normally won't have any of the bad behaviors associated with unneutered male dogs, including the mounting or humping behaviors, the marking of territory, escaping from the yard to find a bitch in season, and fighting. There is really isn't a good reason for *not* neutering a male pet.

My Dog Was Well Housetrained but Is Now Having Accidents

The first thing to do is take him to the veterinarian's office for a checkup. Most dogs will not break housetraining for no reason, and often the reason is related to health. A bladder or urinary tract infection will cause excess or frequent urination. A gastrointestinal upset may cause frequent bowel movements.

If your Dachsie gets a clean bill of health from the vet, you can treat it as a training problem.

Why Does My Dachsie Eat Grass?

For many years, experts believed that dogs ate grass to cause themselves to vomit, because some dogs do vomit after eating grass. However, most dogs don't seem to have any trouble vomiting and will do so whenever something doesn't settle well in the stomach, so that explanation doesn't seem to make much sense.

Instead, it seems that many dogs just like some plant material, and fresh, growing grass is attractive to them. When given a chance, many dogs (including mine) will eagerly consume tomatoes, strawberries, apples, carrots, grapes, and many other fruits and vegetables, especially sweet ones.

Although dogs are scientifically classified as carnivores, behaviorally they appear to be omnivores, animals that consume both animal and plant matter.

When My Dachsie Looks at Me, He'll Obey Me, but If He's Not Looking at Me, He Won't

Are you sure he hears you okay? He may have a hearing impairment. Talk to your vet and have his hearing checked.

Sometimes My Dachsie Yelps or Cries When I Pick Him Up

Go to the vet's office quickly. With Dachsies, the first thought is a back problem, but it could also be something in the intestinal tract or even the liver. Go quickly!

Why Does He Lick His Genitals?

Although licking one's genitals doesn't seem to be an attractive behavior from a human perspective, it is a natural action for your Dachsie. Cleanliness is important to continued good health, and your Dachsie licks himself to keep himself clean.

Occasionally, a male dog will take this behavior from simple cleaning to self-pleasure. If this happens, the owner can stop the behavior with a verbal correction, especially if it occurs in public.

Bet You Didn't Know

The individual personal scent secreted by the anal glands is also why dogs smell each other's feces. That personal scent tells them who this was.

Why Do Dogs Smell Each Others' Rear Ends?

This is another behavior that people don't appreciate but is very natural to dogs. Dogs have scent glands on either side of the anus. These glands, called anal glands, contain a scent that is unique to each dog, a small amount of which will be deposited each time the dog has a bowel movement. When greeting each other, dogs will take a sniff at these glands. Think of this as a personal perfume!

Why Does He Drag His Rear End on the Ground?

This behavior is also related to the anal glands. When these glands get full, they get sore and uncomfortable. A dog will sit down and then drag himself using his front legs so these glands are scratched on the ground. Sometimes this is enough to express or empty the glands.

If full anal glands are not relieved, they can get infected and impacted, sometimes badly enough to require surgery. If your dog is dragging himself on the ground, take him in to see your veterinarian. A dog dragging his rear on the ground could also have intestinal worms that are irritating him. Watch his stool for rice-like segments of tapeworms or take a stool sample in to your vet for analysis.

Dogs Wrestle, So Why Is It Bad for Me to Wrestle with Him?

Dogs wrestle to play. This play prepares puppies for adult life by teaching them social rules (how hard to bite and how far to push the game) and at the same time, it helps puppies learn to use their muscles. When an adult dog plays with a puppy, the game is just as much about learning as it is about fun.

However, when people wrestle with dogs, we play differently. We cannot correct puppies the same way an adult dog can, nor do we communicate with the puppy or young dog in the same way. As a result, by wrestling with us and getting away with behavior he would not be allowed to do to an adult dog, the dog learns to take advantage of us. A bad lesson!

We do not want our dogs to learn they can bite us or use their strength against us; therefore, do not wrestle with your dog!

What Should My Dachsie's Nose Feel Like?

His nose should not be dry and chapped; if it is, call your veterinarian. However, a dog's nose feels cold because of the moisture that evaporates off the nose. His body temperature is actually higher than ours, so if there is no evaporation, his nose will feel warm to us.

Canine Mythology and Other Stuff

There are many old wives' tales and urban myths concerning dogs. Some have a basis in reality, but many are very much fairy tales.

In addition, Dachsies (and other dogs, too, of course) often do things that don't seem to make sense to us. However, Dachsies are sensible animals, and everything they do has a very good reason—to them! As much as we try to understand, sometimes it's difficult to figure out why; but we can try to look at things from your Dachsie's perspective.

Let's take a look at some of the most common canine myths and strange behaviors.

Does One Year of a Dog's Life Really Equal Seven Human Years?

No, that's not really true. A 1-year-old dog is roughly the equivalent (mentally, physically, and sexually) of a 16-year-old human. After that, each year of your dog's life roughly equals about five to seven years of human life. Dachsies, as a small- (minis) to medium- (standards) size dog, will usually live 13 to 16 years.

My Dachsie Likes My Cat!

Many dogs and cats live happily together, especially when raised together. I have three cats and three dogs and have had dogs and cats together for many years. When the dog is taught as a puppy to respect cats and to not chase them, the two species can live together quite nicely.

Dachshund puppies normally need to be taught not to chase cats. Sometimes the cat can do this by swatting the puppy's nose. However, sometimes this just makes a tenacious Dachsie more eager to get the cat. In these cases, the dog must be taught that chasing is not allowed. Once that lesson is learned, dog and cat can both live together in peace and harmony.

My Dachsie Eats Cat Feces!

Ah, the cat litter candy problem! Cats evolved to eat prey, the whole prey, including skin, small bones, meat, and guts. Commercial cat food includes meat but also contains grains and grain products that cats often don't digest well. Therefore, they often pass through only partially digested food, and your Dachsie, smelling this, thinks this is a wonderful treat!

When he helps himself, though, and you get all excited, it becomes a *really* exciting treat; because, after all, you are excited!

Put the cat litter box somewhere where the cats can get into it but the Dachsie can't. Simple prevention is the cure here because you aren't going to change your cats' digestive systems, and the Dachsie is going to continue to search for kitty treats!

If a neighborhood cat is using your yard or garden as a litter box, that's another problem altogether. You are going to have to keep the cat out of your yard because again, if the Dachsie can get to the cat feces, he will!

Watch Out!
Cat feces combined with cat litter could cause serious harm to your dog's digestive tract, potentially even a bowel obstruction. Para-sites and diseases could also be passed from the cat to your dog.

Why Is Chaining a Dog So Bad?

I would rather see you build a dog run—an enclosed fenced area—for your Dachsie rather than chain him. A chained dog is restricted yet vulnerable. He can't get away should a stray dog or other wild animals decide to torment or tease him. Even in a small dog run, he is protected by the fence.

A chained dog also gets very frustrated at his limited movements, and this can cause aggressive behavior. If a small child walks within his reach, the child could bear the brunt of his frustration and could be seriously bitten.

A chained Dachsie will cry, whine, howl, or bark to express his displeasure. He may pace, dig up the dirt around him, or even mutilate himself. In addition, there is the physical damage that happens to the dog's neck by constantly pulling on the end of the chain.

However, even if you have a well-designed dog run, your Dachsie should spend as little time in the run as possible. As I have mentioned many times in this book, a Dachsie must have as much time with his people as possible. A solitary Dachsie is an unhappy dog.

Why Does My Dachsie Stare at Me?

Your dog is probably staring at you to make you do something. Because it is your house and you should be asking him to do things, not vice versa, when he gives you the eye, simply tell him that's enough.

Can a Dachsie Live with Other Pets?

Dachshunds can learn to live with other pets, but you must take care to protect the pets. Rabbits, ferrets, guinea pigs, and other small pets should be securely caged where the Dachsie cannot torment, chase, or harass them. Then, when the Dachsie and other pets are introduced, the Dachsie should be on leash. Interactions between the dog and pets should be strictly supervised. Never allow the dog and pets to be free together unsupervised.

When My Spouse Gives Me a Hug and a Kiss, My Dachsie Tries to Get Between Us

Ah, jealousy! Your Dachsie is trying to get some of that affection; and it doesn't matter how much you give him, he'll probably still try to get in between the two of you. That's just how jealousy works. You can, however, correct the behavior. Don't let the Dachsie run your life, or worse yet, ruin your love life! There is another reason to stop this behavior—as your Dachsie matures, this simple jealousy could turn into protective jealousy. Your Dachsie may start growling when your spouse tries to hug you. A dog that tries to protect you from your spouse could be a real problem!

Why Does He Try to Smell My Crotch?

Your Dachsie smells your crotch because it is part of you and smells like you. Your Dachsie has no social taboos about the crotch area; in fact, to your Dachsie that's a very natural place to sniff. You can, of course, and should, correct him every time he tries to sniff you or other people. Use your voice, "Acckk! No sniff!" and move his nose away.

Why Does My Female Dachsie Hump My Friend's Male Dog?

Your Dachsie is just expressing dominance over the male dog. There are many ways of showing dominance, and this is one way. Very dominant females will often continue this behavior into adulthood, mounting subordinate males during play time. You can stop the behavior when it happens if it bothers you, but it is normal and is not related to a sexual act.

Why Does My Dachsie Bury the Bone I Give Her?

Most dogs bury bones when they are through chewing them. Burying the bone hides it from other predators and protects it for future use.

This behavior probably has its roots in hunting behavior, when survival depended on what was caught during the hunt. Every scrap of meat or bone was important.

Will a Training Collar Hurt My Dachsie?

Most puppies start training on a buckle collar. This is flat, doesn't slip or tighten, and is the correct collar for most puppies. However, at some point many puppies do need more correction and, for these puppies, a training collar can be the right collar.

A training collar (choke chain) will not hurt your Dachsie if it is used properly. Always take it off your dog when you're not closely supervising him. Never allow him to pull the collar tight, and don't try to hold him in place with the collar, which also pulls it tight. If he's gasping or choking, the collar is too tight and is not being used correctly.

Watch Out!
The snap of the leash must be appropriate to the size and age of your Dachsie. It should just tighten and release enough so your Dachsie looks at you in response.

This collar works with a snap and release correction, just enough snap to tighten on the neck with an immediate release. Most of the effect comes from the sound of the chain moving toward the snap. It is never to be used alone, either. Use the snap as you tell the dog what he did wrong.

Remember, there are a variety of training tools you can use. You are not limited to just a training collar (choke chain).

Why Does My Dachsie Still Pull on the Leash Even When He's Choking Himself?

Dogs aren't people, even though we've made them a part of our families, and they don't think like people. Your Dachsie is often so focused on going somewhere to see something, he isn't thinking about the discomfort on his neck. That's why we need to teach him to walk properly so he can go places without choking himself.

My Dachsie Behaves Fine at Home; Why Do We Need a Dog Training Class?

A dog training class is not just for "bad" dogs, it's for all dogs. I'm sure there's still more you can learn even though your Dachsie is good. The instructor will still have information that might be of benefit to you. I have had people attend my dog training classes with their third, fourth, or fifth dogs, and they tell me they learn something new each time.

In addition, a dog training class teaches your dog to be good and pay attention while there are distractions. If you train only at home, your dog will be good only at home. However, when your Dachsie learns to be good with distractions, you can take him many more places.

Why Can't He Sleep with Me?

There is no reason why your Dachsie can't sleep in the room with you, but he needs his own bed. After all, it's your house, you are taking the place of his mother, and you must be his leader as well as his friend. Puppies sleep with their littermates who are their equal, not their mother, who is their leader. Therefore, you need your bed, and he needs his own.

Once your puppy grows up, it's even more important that he has his place. His bed becomes his place of refuge, a place to hide away when life is too exciting or when he has a tummy ache. In addition, you need your own place and, as his leader, you deserve his respect.

You can put his crate in your room, but make him sleep in his crate or bed, and you sleep in yours.

I'm Trying to Train My Dachsie, but He Doesn't Pay Attention!

There are several things that could be happening. First of all, before you even start training, does your Dachsie get enough exercise? If not, paying attention to you could be hard. Does he get enough time with you when you aren't trying to train him? Play time and time for grooming and cuddling are all important.

When you are training, use some really good food treats to teach your Dachsie to pay attention. Then keep the training sessions short and sweet so you aren't asking more than he can give you. Five minutes at a time is more than enough for most young Dachsies.

With my dogs, I will train for a few minutes and then play. Then I will train again for a few minutes and finish up with another play time. My dogs learn that their concentration and attention is rewarded by play time.

My Dog Does Well with His Training for a While and Then Ignores Me

Keep your training sessions short and sweet, and keep varying the positive reinforcements. Use different food treats, toys, squeaky toys, or balls. The easiest way to lose your dog's attention is to bore him!

Is It Okay to Stay Mad at My Dachsie for Doing Something Wrong?

You cannot hold a grudge! When your dog makes a mistake, correct him when you catch him in the act and then prevent that same mistake from happening again. You cannot go around all evening grumbling and complaining. He does not understand why you are angry so long.

My Dachsie Has Lots of Toys, So Why Does He Still Chew on My Stuff?

You may have given your Dachsie too many toys. If he is surrounded by toys, he learns that everything is his and he can play with and chew on everything! However, if you limit his toys and only give him two or three at a time, he learns that only some things are his.

Take away a few of his toys. When he touches something of yours, let him know that's wrong, "Acckk! No!" Take it away and hand him one of his toys, "Here, this is yours!"

Keep in mind, too, that your Dachsie may be chewing on your stuff because it's yours and he likes your smell (which is on your stuff). With these dogs, prevention is the key. Put your stuff away and don't let your Dachsie have too much freedom.

Understanding Hunting Behavior

Hunting dogs are found in many different sizes, body shapes, and skills. Dachshunds, as we know, were designed to be able to move quickly through brush, go down burrows, and be tenacious enough to find and hold their prey. This requires an athletic dog with a strong, agile body, powerful but short legs, and a strong personality.

Both hearing and scent are important to hunting dogs, as is sight. Sight, however, is keyed more to movement than to recognizing objects that are not moving. This is why your Dachsie reacts more to a bird flying overhead than to the bird perched quietly on the fence.

Hunting dogs have a very strong instinct to chase anything that moves. Birds, a cat, a rolling ball, a thrown Frisbee, or even a moving car will all kick-start that chase instinct. That means you must be aware of it and protect your Dachsie from himself.

The Least You Need to Know

- Dogs aren't people, and their body language, instincts, and behaviors are different.

- Dogs do things for a reason. We may not understand why, but they do.

- It's important that we know as much about our dogs as we can so we can make both our lives more enjoyable and safer.

- Dachshunds were originally hunting dogs and retain many of those instincts.

A Doggy Dictionary

aggression   A hostile reaction to stimuli. It can be directed toward people, dogs, or other things. Aggression is the fight part of the fight or flight instinct.

agility   An obstacle course for dogs that can be used for fun training and confidence or as a competitive sport.

allergies   A bodily reaction to a substance that is touched, inhaled, or ingested. The body then releases histamines (hence an antihistamine to treat it). Dogs can have allergies just as people can and often to the same things.

alternative behavior   Any action (or inaction) you train your dog to perform in order to prevent an unwanted behavior.

American Kennel Club (AKC)   The AKC registers litters of puppies and individual dogs and licenses dog shows and other dog events.

anticipation   When a dog reacts before you give a command, he knows what's going to happen next.

Be still   An obedience command for holding still.

body language   Your dog's use of body position, body parts, and facial expressions to communicate.

bonding   A feeling of deep commitment or attraction between dog and owner; a responsibility toward each other.

boundary training   Teaching the dog to remain within and to respect boundaries.

buckle collar   A wide nylon, cotton, or leather collar that fastens with a buckle.

Canine Good Citizen   A program administered by the AKC to promote good canine citizens and responsible owners.

choke collar   Training collar, works with a snap and release motion. Also called choke chain.

Come   An obedience command for the dog to stop everything and come directly to you.

conformation competition   Dog shows for evaluating a dog as compared to others of his breed and in accordance with breed standards.

correction   Verbal or physical acknowledgment of a mistake.

CPR (Cardiac Pulmonary Resuscitation)   An emergency first-aid procedure to keep your dog's heart beating and to keep breath in him.

cue   Command, signal.

distractions   Things that can break the dog's concentration.

dominance   Levels of comfort within the pack or family group.

earth dog   Same as go to ground; field trials for Dachshunds and Terriers in which the dog goes into a tunnel after prey.

emergency   A medical or veterinary emergency is something that is life threatening and cannot wait until the next business day.

exercise   Physical activity or the movement in reaction to a command.

fearful aggression   An aggressive reaction by a timid or shy dog that is caused by fear.

field trial   A trial or evaluation for sporting dogs.

force   Making the dog do what you want; using physical strength.

go to ground   Field trials for Terriers and Dachshunds in which the dog goes into a tunnel after prey. Also called earth dog.

group classes   Small group situations in which dogs and owners are taught by an obedience instructor.

halter   A training tool that fits over the dog's head much like a horse's halter; it can be used instead of a training collar.

heartworm   A parasitic worm that lives in the heart; left untreated it causes death.

Heel   An obedience command for having a dog walk by your left side, with his neck and shoulders by your left leg.

hip dysplasia   A deformity of the hip.

hookworm   An intestinal parasite.

housetraining   Teaching the puppy to relieve itself outside, not in the house.

instinct   Inborn urges to respond to things in a specific manner.

leash awareness   Teaching the dog to be aware of the leash and owner, to respect the leash.

Let's go   An obedience command for having a dog walk nicely on the leash without pulling; not the Heel command.

long line   A longer length of leash or clothesline rope used as a training tool for the Come command and for boundary training.

lure   Something to encourage the dog to follow, to be shaped into position, or to do something.

Lyme disease   A tick-transmitted disease.

mimic   To learn by watching and then copying another's actions.

motivation   A dog's desire to do something or obey a command; can be influenced by providing a reward.

motivator   A reward or lure for doing something right.

negative attention   Corrections that are purposefully sought by the dog (by misbehaving) as a means of getting attention from the owner.

parasite   An organism that lives off another.

pinch or prong collar   A multi-linked training collar that pinches instead of chokes.

positive reinforcement   Anything positive used to encourage a dog to continue behaving or obeying commands; can include verbal praise, petting, food treats, and toys.

praise   Verbal affirmation, approval.

Rocky Mountain spotted fever   A tick-transmitted disease.

shaping   Using a training tool to help the dog do what you want; shaping into position.

shock   A life-threatening condition caused by a trauma.

Sit   An obedience command for having a dog get into a sitting position, with his hips down and front end up.

socialization   The process of introducing a puppy to different people, sights, sounds, and smells.

Stay   An obedience command for having a dog hold his position without moving.

submissive   Showing respect for dominance.

temperament   Personality and character.

therapy dogs   Trained and certified dogs who visit people in nursing homes and hospitals.

time out   Time away from training that gives the dog a chance to rest and think; it breaks the thought process, especially if the dog has been misbehaving.

tourniquet   A device used to stop major blood flow after an injury.

training tools   Anything you use to train your dog, including leash and collar, food treats, and your voice.

vaccination   Injections that encourage the body to develop antibodies to protect from specific diseases.

Wait   An obedience command for holding still and waiting for another command.

Appendix B

Dachshunds (and Other Dogs) on the Internet

The Internet has become a wonderful research tool for dog lovers. Dachsie owners can find a tremendous amount of information specifically about their breed and about dogs in general. You can also use it to purchase supplies, including dog food, grooming tools, and toys.

A word of warning is in order, however: *Never* assume that just because it's on the Internet the information or advice is correct. Anyone can post a web page, and although there is good information out there, there's also a lot of garbage! Don't hesitate to ask more questions, and look at who is doing the writing.

Specifically Dachshunds

www.dachshundrescue.org
Dachsie rescue, including frequently asked questions about the breed

www.c2cdr.org
Coast to Coast Dachsie rescue

www.drna.org
Dachsie rescue of North America

www.drwp.net
Dachshund rescue web page

www.dachshund-dca.org
Dachshund Club of America

www.calabel.net/guidetodachshundtitles.htm
A guide to titles that Dachsies can earn and a guide to Dachsie abbreviations

www.dachshund-dca.org/versatility_certificate
Explains the Dachshund Club of America's Versatility program

www.abledogs.net
A site for the owners of disabled dogs

www.dachsie.org
For the love of Dachsies!

www.dachshund-dca.org/diskbook
Canine Disk Disease explained

www.akc.org
American Kennel Club

www.akc.org/breeds/recbreeds/dach.cfm
AKC Dachshund breed standard

Nutrition and Health

www.petinsurance.com
Veterinary Pet Insurance

www.navigator.tufts.edu
Nutritional Navigator; for more information about nutrition

www.quackwatch.com
A site about human medicine designed to help people avoid "quackery" or false information; very informative for dog owners, too

www.petnet.com
Pfizer Animal Health; includes information about dog and cat health care as well as emergency first aid

www.goodpet.com
Dr. Goodpet Laboratories; a major supplier of natural pet products

www.canidae.com
Canidae Pet Foods

www.hillspet.com
Hill's Pet Nutrition, Inc.

www.iamsco.com
Iams Co. dog and pet foods

www.naturzchoice.com
Nature's Choice dog foods

www.petconnect.com/nutro
Nutro Products

www.purina.com
Purina dog food

www.waltham.com
Waltham dog foods

General and Miscellaneous Information

www.kitten.com/dogs
Purina dog and cat pages; have a lot of different information of interest to dog owners, including grooming information

www.cbs.com/lateshow/ttlist
Search for "dogs" to get David Letterman's top 10 lists concerning dogs

www.animalnetwork.com
Fancy Publications, including *Dog Fancy* and *Dogs USA*

kao.ini.cmu.edu:5500/bdf
Blue Dog, a site for kids; specifically teaching kids elementary math skills

www.familyinternet.com/pet/apdt
Association of Pet Dog Trainers

www.kimberly.uidaho.edu/nadoi
National Association of Dog Obedience Instructors

www.canismajor.com/dog/guide
Dog Owner's Guide

www.dualcom.com/books/dogs
Books about dogs

www.amazon.com
A big bookstore with lots of dog books

Dog Supplies—Including Toys and Grooming Tools

www.caninequp.com
Canine Equipment; as they put it, "gear fer dogs"; ask for catalog

www.foxandhounds.com
Fox and Hound Ltd.; a pet supplier and a manufacturer of pet collars

www.blueribbonpet.com
Blue Ribbon Pet Supplies

www.cardinalpet.com
Cardinal Laboratories; pet supplies, including shampoos

www.coastalpet.com
Coastal Pet Products; sells supplies, including collars and leashes

Email: dogtreats@aol.com
Desert Dog Treat Co.; e-mail for information on great homemade dog treats

www.happydogtoys.com
Happy Dog Toys

www.fourpaws.com
Four Paws Products

www.flexiusa.com
Flexi USA, Inc.; retractable leashes

www.hydrosurge.com
Hydrosurge, Inc.; grooming supplies and shampoos

www.midwesthomes4pets.com
Midwest Homes for Pets; kennel crates and more

www.kongcompany.com
Kong Co.; toys

www.lambertkay.com
Lambert Kay; shampoos and more

www.4dogs.com
Supplies and treats

www.sitstay.com/store/toys
Dog toys

www.pet-expo.com
JB Wholesale; toys and supplies

www.puptents.com
Dog supplies

www.dogbeds.com
Dog supplies, including beds and leashes

www.jbpet.com
J-B Pet Supplies; ask for their catalog

www.jandjdog.com
J & J Supplies; competitive obedience and agility supplies

Index

C